Parisian Life

Adventures in
The City of Light

Edith
de Belleville

ISBN 978-1-66783-198-5 (Print)

ISBN 978-1-66783-199-2 (eBook)

Preface

I NEVER UNDERSTOOD WHY WRITERS WRITE A PREFACE. IF THE book is good, why would you need a preface? To me, it's like if you go to the supermarket, and each time you want to buy a product, someone jumps out and says, "Hey! You! Buy my product. It's the best!"

But Lisa (my good friend from New York who lives in Paris, and wrote a good book), told me, "Edith in the U.S., it's common to write a preface. And for you, it's important to tell American women that you are on their side, and that's why you wrote your book." Lisa knows, so I do what Lisa says.

I wrote this book because I'm annoyed by all the books written for the U.S. market that tell my American sisters how they need to be as slim, sexy, refined, young-looking (without plastic surgery), the best mother, and of course, as chic as a French woman—or even better, a Parisian woman. Enough is enough! We should support each other, we women from all over the world, instead of feeling we must conform to some marketing directive: "If you can't be a French woman, at least try to imitate her."

As a woman born, raised, educated, married (and divorced) in Paris, I say "non!" Stay as you are!

I wrote this book to share my beloved city, and tell how history, poetry, literature—and Paris—can make you the heroine in your own story.

But as you are, not as a Parisian. Because living in Paris is a privilege.

I hope you will enjoy this journey in The City of Light with me. By the way, if someone knows how French women can look young without plastic surgery, I'd love to know.

—Edith de Belleville, Paris

Table of Contents

Chapter 1:

Lost with Napoléon

CLICK-CLACK, CLICK-CLACK, CLICK-CLACK.

I'm walking on the pavement of the beautiful courtyard of the Hôtel des Invalides, a building from the seventeenth century. I don't know if you have ever walked on cobblestones in high heels, but believe me, it's not easy at all.

If it were a different day, I would be explaining to you that this magnificent place was built by Louis the XIV, our glorious Sun King. You can't miss Les Invalides; it's the golden dome that you see on postcards of Paris. The Sun King wanted a shelter for his soldiers who were injured during the 32 years of wars against almost all of Europe. The injured soldiers were invalids; that's where the name "Invalides" comes from. The architects, Liberal Bruand and Hardouin-Mansart, found inspiration in the Spanish royal palace, El Escorial, in Madrid. Now Les Invalides is a military hospital and museum.

Where does my knowledge about Paris come from? I'm a native Parisian and a licensed tour guide. But right now, I'm not in the mood to be your tour guide. It's midnight; I'm all alone, and I just want to get out of here. There's no light, I'm cold, tired, and lost. Absolutely lost.

I know what you're thinking: how can a Parisian, who's supposed to do guided tours of Les Invalides, get lost? It's my weakness. I have no sense of direction. For a tour guide, I know it's not exactly convenient. A Swedish friend of mine told me it's not my fault because women have no sense of direction (I know, un peu sexiste), so he gave me a compass. It's a perfectly good gold compass, but it's useless since I have no idea how to use it. I've done many guided tours of Les Invalides, of course, but during the day. But now it's very dark and I can't see a thing.

Where is the exit? I go to the right side of the courtyard, next to the big arcades. There are magnificent, old canons but no gate. I go to the left side—click-clack, click-clack—the place is vast. No exit.

I look up, and that's when I see him.

The full moon highlights his slim silhouette. He looks young, not very tall, but he has charisma in his military uniform. Behind him, I see the golden dome of the Invalides, which shines.

He is watching me, this man. I recognize him; you can't miss him with his signature bicorn hat. It's Napoléon Bonaparte.

"Hey, you!" I scream in the direction of the statue of Napoleon. "Yes, you! The little Corsican! Tell me where the exit is!"

No answer.

"You don't know?" I shout. "Or you don't want to tell me?" I'm not surprised. I never liked Napoleon, anyway. First of all, he was a misogynist and a bad lover. Five minutes, tops. He had more lovers than battles. And he was terrible to sweet, devoted Joséphine. "Plus, you sent thousands of young soldiers to die for your enormous ego!"

I sigh. I should have not drunk so much Champagne. Now, I feel dizzy, and I have a headache. This chilling cold, these canons all around, and this statue of Bonaparte remind me of a poem by Victor Hugo. It's about the disastrous Russian Campaign of Napoléon in the winter of 1812. To cheer myself, I think of these beautiful verses. Well, to be honest, I try to remember the verses of Hugo, which is about as easy as walking on cobblestones in high-heels.

Ah yes…I remember now. More or less.

It snowed.
Someone was defeated by his conquest.
For the first time, the eagle lowered its head.
Heavy days!
Men discarded cannons
Who lay down, died
Ten of thousands went to sleep, a hundred awoke, it snowed
it snowed always, the cold wind…

The wind is very cold here, too. I'm freezing half to death; I'm wearing only a white silk blouse with a pencil skirt, and an elegant (but not very warm) black jacket. I'm starting to panic. I'm going to die of cold exactly like the thousands of Napoleon's poor soldiers in Russia.

How did I get an invitation at midnight to this prestigious courtyard? Me, who is not even a VIP? Mrs. Nobody? Well, it's a long story.

• • •

It all started at a party.

I was invited to this party by Randy, a friendly Francophile doctor from Los Angeles who comes to Paris twice a year. It was a potluck, so I brought the only thing I know how to make chocolate mousse. I'm always successful with my chocolate mousse. The secret is not to add sugar (yes, none at all) and to use the very best dark chocolate.

While the guests were eating the desserts, a woman came over to compliment me on my mousse. Her tight green jeans, her black linen jacket and her stilettos were highlighting her tall silhouette. Her big, dark eyes underlined with kohl pencil were perfectly fitting with her curly, short black hair. She had allure! She was probably my age, meaning in her fifties.

Her name was Marie-Jeanne. She explained how she became a choc-olate addict. It was hard to believe, because this woman was extremely slim. She was warm and charming, and for a moment, I thought she might be American since she spoke fluent English with what seemed like an American accent.

Not at all. Turns out, she was Corsican, and she told me that she was teaching American History at the prestigious Political Sciences Institute, or Sciences Po, as they call it here in Paris.

During this time, I was trying to write a book about the great Parisian women of history and what today's women can learn from them. But I was doubting myself a lot because I doubt a lot in general. Was it a good idea? Was it really a new concept? Does the world need yet another book about Parisian women?

I was sharing all my doubts with the friendly Marie-Jeanne when she said to me:

"Oh! I know who you should meet! My good friend Jean who is a historian! He's an expert on the seventeenth century. He'll tell you if your book idea is good or not."

Of course, I knew him. This "Jean" is professor at the prestigious Sorbonne, and even appears on TV programs.

"But do you really think he'll have time to see me and to give me his advice?" I ask Marie-Jeanne, wondering why this famous, busy French his-torian would care about me and my unwritten "masterpiece."

"His family comes from the same little village in Corsica as mine," she says, "So if I ask him, yes, he will meet you. He won't have a choice!"

She compliments me again on my "killer" chocolate mousse, as she takes another bite of her third helping. I tell her how grateful I am to have met her. Really grateful.

• • •

Cling!

A text message: "Good morning, I'm Jean Pasqualini, historian, the friend of Marie-Jeanne. She told me you wanted to meet me. Where and when?"

Talk about a direct message. I can tell this man has no time to lose. To be honest, I was sure that Marie-Jeanne would never contact him, and even if she did, I was sure he would never contact me (I'm a bit of a pessimist). But obviously Marie-Jeanne liked me and my chocolate mousse was enough to convince this professor to write to me one month later.

Where and when? Okay, let me think, Mister Famous Historian. When? Tomorrow. And where? Yes, of course, I know where!

I reply: "Tomorrow at 10:30 a.m. at Le Bonaparte Café."

Cling! His answer: "Alright. See you tomorrow." With a smiley face emoji.

At least he has a sense of humor; he understood my joke. What better for a Corsican historian than to meet in a café called Le Bonaparte on Rue Bonaparte?

Fortunately, Le Bonaparte Café is next to the Saint-Germain-des-Prés Metro station. I could have chosen the mythical Café de Flore—cradle of writers, intellectuals, and poets from the nineteenth century. But for my important meeting, I preferred a simpler café, nothing ostentatious. Paris cafés are like the Parisian inhabitants. Each one has its own style, its own personality.

I love Paris cafés. I spend half my life in the cafés of Paris. Since I was 15 years old, I have been going to a café every day.

Parisian cafes are where I celebrate good times, and where I insulate myself from bad news. It's where I've had love at first sight, but also where I've had break-ups and cried. Cafes are, for me, the place to be when I want to be alone but not feel alone.

Paris would not be Paris without its cafés. The soul of Paris is in its cafés. Cafés were the laboratory of ideas where writers, artists, and intellectuals invented movements that all end in -ism: Impressionism, Romanticism,

Surrealism, Cubism and Existentialism. A Paris café is also where a wanderer ends his or her aimless stroll. It's where you meet your friend for a coffee and chat. It's where you have your business meeting or your rendezvous with your lover. It's also where you do nothing but people-watch.

Le Bonaparte Café is less prestigious than Café de Flore, of course, but has lots of charm. It's a small café, doesn't get too crowded, and the old engravings of Paris on its walls give you a homey feeling. While you sip your coffee, you can chat with the friendly waiters, and enjoy the best view of the Church of Saint-Germain-des-Prés.

I can see the colorful chairs of the terrace, which are empty and waiting for me, and the canopy with its blue and burgundy stripes. But to access the elegant terrace, I need to first cross a tiny square, Place Jean-Paul Sartre and Simone de Beauvoir, which is full of cobblestones. You won't find it on Google Maps but I know it is there. I walk slowly in my high-heeled leather sandals.

The sun is shining, the sky is blue, and it's not too cold for December, so I sit on the terrace. I'm wearing a purple dress, a purple velvet jacket, and purple tights. I like purple. Colors give me energy, and this morning I really need positive vibes.

Boom, boom, boom. I can hear my heartbeat. My belly hurts. I'm anxious. This morning is very important for me, because the book I want to write is a lifelong goal. I'm worried what this famous historian will think about my idea.

The idea first came to me while giving lectures about famous Parisian women in history. I'd been giving lectures in cafés about these women for a while. And little by little, these fantastic women became my life coaches. Sarah Bernhardt, George Sand, Joséphine de Beauharnais, Madame de Montespan, and Christine de Pisan speak to me, and share their wisdom when I feel lost. With their guidance, I feel more free, audacious—and more like me. Finally, I decided to write a book explaining what these great Parisiennes from the past can teach us 21st-century women. What were their tools of success? How can we follow their path today? This is what my book is about. But how will I react if this French history expert tells me that my idea is naïve, or stupid? What will happen if he says my concept has been done to death?

Or if his eyes say: how dare you write about French history—you, who are not even an historian?

I need to relax, but I'm too nervous to read the book I have in my bag, or even look at the screen on my smartphone. So, I look around me. Embrace the world! I tell myself as a mantra to give me some courage.

Alright, embracing the world…

I'm breathing, watching, and hearing what's around me. Ding-dong, ding-dong. The bells of Saint-Germain-des-Prés are saying it's ten o'clock in the morning. For over a thousand years those bells have been telling Parisians the time of day. From where I am sitting, I can admire this medieval church. Before the era of Jean-Paul Sartre and Simone de Beauvoir, the district of Saint-Germain-des-Prés was already a home for the Literati.

Paris is such a lively history book. As I survey Rue Bonaparte, I realize that this street, too, is a history book—an art history book. The prestigious Ecole des Beaux-Arts (the fine arts school) is located here.

Les Beaux Arts were, and still are, the Holy Grail for any art student. But at one time, a few young rebels refused to study in this conservative art school. They were the Impressionists of the 19th century. Claude Monet, Auguste Renoir, Frederic Bazille, Berthe Morisot, Camille Pissaro, Edgar Degas, Gustave Caillebotte who worshipped and admired their master Edouard Manet.

The master suffered a lot. While I'm drinking my coffee, I think that it's always the same story. All his life, Manet wanted glory, but he received only disdain from the narrow-minded French. Manet created the most scandalous painting of all art history, a naked woman lying on her bed and waiting for her lover-client. The painting is called "Olympia" and you can see it at the Musée d'Orsay, here in Paris. And guess where Manet was born? In Rue Bonaparte—just near the conservative school of fine arts that rejected him, and that he hated all his life. Ironic, isn't it?

I'm observing my table neighbors. An American couple—(I recognize their delightful southern accent)—probably retired because they're not young. I like observing people in cafés. I always try to imagine their stories.

That's why I never go to Starbucks. Don't get me wrong, I have nothing against Starbucks. Starbucks cafés are comfortable, the toilets are clean, the staff is friendly, and they have great coffee. But at Starbucks, I feel lonely. Everybody is so serious: mute, focused on their computers or smartphones. Having a coffee in Starbucks is like having coffee in a library. Nobody chats, and they ignore me. I also don't like having to give someone my name just to pick up my coffee. And I hate—but really hate—drinking my coffee in a cardboard cup with a wooden stick while being forced to listen to loud elevator music. When I drink my coffee, I need a real cup and a real spoon, like an adult.

This American couple is so close to me that I can smell their croissants. I should have eaten something, but I'm too stressed to swallow anything. I'm wondering how these two charming tourists would react if I told them that on this exact spot where they're enjoying their crispy croissants, a bomb destroyed the Bonaparte Café. That was when writer/ philosopher Jean-Paul Sartre used to live in a third-floor apartment on Rue Bonaparte, just next to this café. Sartre was a supporter of Algerian independence, a colony of France since 1830. In 1962, an extremist group put a bomb in his apartment. Fortunately, the philosopher was not killed, but the café was destroyed. The distraught owner was heard to say, "They couldn't shoot him in the street like everyone else?"

The way the American couple talk to each other tells me that, even at their age, they are still in love. Like Sartre and Simone de Beauvoir. Sartre and Beauvoir are the Bonnie and Clyde of philosophy. Philosophers and lovers. Free love, never married, and committed to each other despite the many other lovers they had. It's so Rock and Roll. Then, at 40 years old, Sartre finally decided to move in with a woman. With Simone? No. One of his other younger and prettier lovers? Not at all. For 17 years, Sartre lived with his mommy at 42 Rue Bonaparte. Big, important men are so disappointing when you realize that they are just little boys inside.

And speaking of famous men…I see mine coming toward the café, Mister Famous History Professor. Boom, boom, boom…

He's wearing a black coat with a white woolen scarf around his neck. He walks quickly across the plaza. Oh! He is taller than on TV. He must be in his sixties. I wave to him since he can't recognize me.

As he's coming toward me, I examine his face. An aquiline nose and a well-drawn mouth and hazelnut eyes. Exactly my kind of man—slim, smart, and charming. He shakes my hand, saying through a beautiful smile, "Bonjour Madame."

I shake his hand, returning the smile "Bonjour Monsieur Pasqualini," I say. "I'm so grateful that you took the time to see me."

"You're welcome," he says with sparkling eyes. "Any friend of Marie-Jeanne is a friend of mine."

I can't tell if he means it, or just being charming. He apologizes for not having a lot of time for me. "So, tell me about your book." He gets right to it.

He orders a coffee, then turns his full attention to me. He's not such a scary man, I tell myself to steady my nerves. He has the friendly, sing-song accent of the south. He's a nice man. But he's also an impressive man, a renowned history professor. I stutter as I explain my book concept. I'm trying to sum up and not waste his precious time, but it's making it worse. I can't find the right words. Suddenly, I'm back in my university days, trying to pass an oral exam for a PhD in history.

Voilà, finally it's over, it's done.

The professor doesn't say a word. He just takes a deep breath, turning his spoon in his coffee.

Finally, he turns to me, narrowing his brown eyes. "So, you're the Joan of Arc of history? Hearing voices of dead women who give you advice?"

Thwack! I feel like he's slapped me. Joan of Arc? Is that an insult?

I'm dazed. I can feel that I'm flushed. Alright, he's making fun of me, and my book. I'm speechless. My idea of using history as a coaching method is stupid.

I suddenly need air. I can feel my cheeks burning up and my hands becoming moist. I drink a sip of water to calm down. I contract in my chair, grip my handbag. I put on a fake grin to hide the pain of his sarcastic dig, but my lips are pinched. I feel my face collapse.

"Excellent idea!" I hear him say.

Wait—did he just say it was an excellent idea? Am I dreaming?

Before I can ask, he stands up to leave. "I'm very sorry, but I have to go. I have to prepare a history lecture for next week." He offers to buy my coffee. "It was a pleasure to meet you, madame. You're a brilliant woman. You know, intelligence is a tool of seduction for a woman," he says with a grin. "Good luck with your book."

I'm so surprised by his compliments that I can only answer, "Merci!"

Just before leaving, he turns back to me. "Since you seem interested in Napoléon, why don't you attend my lecture next Saturday evening? It's about his enemy." He hands me a flyer then walks off.

I'm left alone with my empty cup. Brilliant woman, indeed. Could I not have come up with something smarter than "Merci?" I sigh into my coffee. How stupid I am. Why am I so shy? Always the same story; I feel uncomfortable with compliments, as if I don't deserve them. But "merci" was the only word I was able to say.

Oh well. I take a deep breath and drink my glass of water, savoring the moment. The cool water tastes like Champagne. Everything tastes wonderful. I wave to the waiter and show him my empty coffee cup. Another coffee to celebrate this fantastic news.

Alright, so I haven't written my book yet and I have no idea how to publish it, but I got the green light from a renowned French historian. That's just what I needed to begin writing. I am overflowing with confidence.

I look again at the flyer he gave me: The Association of French History Teachers of the Sorbonne and The Association of Corsicans of Paris are happy to invite you to the lecture of Professor Pasqualini: "Pasquale Paoli, Father of Corsica."

Who is this Paoli? I reflect as I inspect the logo of Café Bonaparte. No idea who he is, but if he was an enemy of Napoléon, he must have a temper. Sounds interesting.

• • •

Clap, clap, clap.

Fifty people in an amphitheater in Les Invalides are applauding the History professor. I didn't even know there was an amphitheater here. I've learned so many things tonight about Pasquale Paoli, the father of Corsica. If you don't know where Corsica is, it's the small triangle-shaped island near the southern coast of France. One day, I'll go to Corsica, which has earned the nickname, "The Isle of Beauty."

Corsica has been part of France since the eighteenth century. It was sold by the Italian city of Genoa to King Louis XV. Anyway, Corsicans never felt like Italians or French, only Corsicans. The Paolis fought for the independence of their homeland. He was a man from the Age of Enlightenment. Full of progressive and modern ideas.

Just as I'm about to leave, I hear the voice of Professor Pasqualini over the loudspeaker: "And now my friends, you are invited to a small buffet." I follow the people across the courtyard of Les Invalides. We take a majestic staircase that leads to a hidden room. I had no idea there was a hidden room in Les Invalides. The room is lit by candlelight and smells of clementine. Incredible! I feel like I'm in another time—in the Age of Enlightenment. There is a buffet filled with the most refined and beautiful dishes.

I try to find the professor to thank him. I finally see him but he's surrounded by people all wanting him to sign his books, so I don't push. I hate to impose myself, and I can see he's busy with his fan club of beautiful women.

I know nobody here, and I'm too shy to talk with the elegant guests, so I make a move to leave. But just as I'm about to go, I hear a deep voice call out to me.

"Edith! I'm so glad you came!" The professor tells me he has to sign a few books but asks me to stay. "Help yourself to the buffet and wait for me please, my dear. We'll talk about your book…and a few other things," he says with a wink and big grin.

Is the charming professor flirting with me? I can tell he likes me. I feel the jealous eyes of his fan club glaring at me behind my back. But I don't mind. I try to walk as elegantly as I can past them, toward the sumptuous buffet.

I order a glass of Champagne. While drinking, I attempt to listen in on the conversation of the two people next to me.

"Of course, Paoli was gay!" one of them says. "How do you explain that he never married? Why don't we know of any of his lovers? For a Corsican man, it's weird, don't you think?" She's talking with conviction to the man beside her. I try to listen to the rest of their conversation, but they move away from the buffet. I can just make out the name Maria Cosway. They're debating whether her relationship with Paoli was romantic or platonic.

Maria Cosway! Of course, I know her. She was the great love of Thomas Jefferson. Maria Cosway had everything—a blond beauty with blue eyes, a talent for music and painting. But she was unhappily married to a horrible Englishman. Thomas Jefferson and Maria met in Paris and had an affair. Well, probably had an affair. They fell in love, for sure, but Jefferson left Paris to return to America. He wrote Maria romantic letters, a dialogue between heart and head. Of course, his head won. Maria Cosway inspired the love of great men: Jefferson and Paoli. Not bad. What a woman!

While I'm interested in history, what I really prefer are the love stories of history. I'm a romantic woman with an imagination. A dreamer. I believe in fairy tales, and history is full of them. You don't need to read fictional love stories when you know history.

Corsicans are famous for having a temper; they are passionate, warm, and friendly. And like me, they love freedom. I love Corsicans. I want to have a Corsican boyfriend. And I'm going to soon. I can feel it. For sure, Mister Pasqualini, the famous historian, has a crush on me. I noticed the way he was watching me at Café Bonaparte. Sure, he stayed only fifteen minutes, but he was in a hurry. He's a busy man, like Napoléon. But he made a point of mentioning that he liked "brilliant" women, and added with sparkling eyes that I was a brilliant woman. Those velvet eyes and pretty mouth said so. QED. And among the sexy and young admirers tonight, he chose me, calling me "my dear" in front of everybody. I feel that my future is going to change.

I'm like Napoléon's Joséphine. When Joséphine de Beauharnais met the Corsican general she was broke. She had no husband, and was not so young anymore. She was raising her two children on her own, trying to survive in a hostile world. Exactly like me. Joséphine had the intuition that Napoléon was her soulmate.

And she was right. They became a tight-knit couple; they helped each other gain success. Joséphine and Napoléon: The Dream Team.

Thanks to her Corsican husband, Josephine became Empress of France. Thanks to the viscountess Joséphine de Beauharnais, Napoléon domesticated the nobles and Royalists who hated him, the "French Revolution's son."

Me too, I have the feeling that my sad past will be soon over thanks to my brilliant Corsican professor. He has seventy published books, so he'll help me to publish mine. Thanks to his wonderful networking, I'm sure that well-known journalists will talk about my book. It'll be a bestseller in France, then Europe. Maybe it will become a Hollywood movie. Who knows? I let my mind wander. I imagine us wintering in our country house in Corsica. We'll write our masterpieces, sharing our thoughts and our love. We will have stimulating conversations near the fireplace while eating Corsican roasted chestnuts. I'm going to become the French Empress of historic novels thanks to my genius general of the literary battlefields.

It's very late. What's he doing? How many books does he have to sign? I drank too much Champagne and my head is spinning. Suddenly, like in a play, a statuesque blond woman appears from a hidden door. She struts across the room, sending a trail of her expensive perfume behind her. Her long, slim fingers are covered with gold rings; her long nails are polished the color of blood.

"Ah! Chériiiii!" she calls out in the direction of the professor.

What? Chéri? Why is she calling my Corsican fiancé "cheri?" Obviously, he's not only mine because she is putting her blood-colored lips on his mouth in front of everyone. He looks very surprised, but doesn't move away, and seems to enjoy it.

I'm choked up. I need to sit.

How naïve and stupid I am! How could I think that I, Mrs. Nobody, who is not a sophisticated and gorgeous Parisian woman with red claws and haute couture clothes, could have an affair with this prestigious man?

I'm a mature woman, so I'm supposed to have a mature mind. But I have the mind of a teenager because I have too much imagination and can be a little naïve when it comes to men. I imagined he had a crush on me just because he was flirting. Pathetic.

Goodbye Corsican fiancé, bestseller, money, and villa in Corsica.

I feel so foolish. I need to get out of here, to forget this Corsican party.

I run away, down the majestic stairs, as fast as I can. I arrive in the courtyard, to the statue of Napoléon. I'm cold, my coat forgotten in the cloakroom. There's no light, I'm cold, tired, and lost. Absolutely lost.

At Waterloo Napoleon did surrender
Oh yeah!
And I have met my destiny in quite similar way
The history book on the shelf
Is always repeating itself

Waterloo
I was defeated, you won the war
Waterloo
Promise to love you forever more
Waterloo
Couldn't escape if I wanted to
Waterloo
Knowing my fate is to be with you
Waterloo
Finally facing my Waterloo

I sing the ABBA song in front of the statue of Napoléon. I'm lost in this place and I'm also lost in my life. My destiny looks like Waterloo. At more than fifty years old, I've failed in everything. I tried to win the battle, but like Napoléon in Waterloo, I am defeated. I feel alone in the world. I struggle to raise my two boys on my own, but it's too hard.

Suddenly, I hear a sound.

I'd love to tell you that this sound is the charismatic history professor coming to save me, telling me breathlessly, "You are the love of my life! I don't care about the other woman!" Like my Prince Charming, arriving with my coat, and I, like Cinderella at midnight, my pumpkin is transformed into an Über coach.

But my life is not a fairy tale, and Paris is not Hollywood. French movies don't have happy endings. The sound I heard is my smartphone, which has fallen onto the pavement.

So, instead of being Cinderella, I decide to be MacGyver. I use my phone as a lamp and, little by little, I find the amphitheater, the cloakroom, and my ugly-but-warm coat. With the light, I even find the exit. At last! As I arrive in front of the huge gate, I stop.

I'm mesmerized by the full moon lighting up the Eiffel Tower just in front of me. On the right, boxwood bushes shaped like canons sit beside actual canons. Behind me, the golden dome sparkles.

All is silence. I'm alone to enjoy this magical moment. It's like this spectacular vision was made just for me. It's like a dream.

A soldier opens the golden door and I walk into the deserted streets in the direction of the Métro, singing ABBA's Waterloo. I feel like I'm on a movie set, or in a film. Paris is magic. I am happy again.

I arrive at the Invalides Métro station, take the line 13. I grab a seat, close my eyes and think. Yes, I'm a clumsy woman. Yes, I'm absent-minded, pessimistic, too sensitive, naïve, stupid sometimes, and I cry at nothing. Yes, I'm a dreamer, and I take my dreams for reality. I live in the past and I'm lost in the present. I'm also tacky from time to time, and I do not understand this modern world.

But I have Paris. Paris is my home. Like the literary monks from the Middle Ages who had their church in Saint-Germain-des-Prés, like the injured soldiers of Louis XIV who had the Hotel des Invalides to protect them, Paris is my shelter. This city is my amniotic fluid

Paris makes me feel everything more potently. Everything done in Paris is more delicious, more powerful. I feel more alive here.

In Paris, my life is like a romance novel. The beauty of this city consoles me when I feel down. The stories of this poetic urban place entertain me when I'm bored. The lively Parisians sitting in the cafés make me smile when I'm sad.

Yes, as long as I have Paris, I'll have hope.

After a few minutes, I open my eyes and see the Métro stop Duroc. A Napoléonic general. Even the subways of Paris can tell you fascinating stories: Hortense, the daughter of Joséphine de Beauharnais from her first marriage, was madly in love with Duroc, a handsome general in Napoléon's army. But Joséphine had other plans for her beloved daughter. "I forbid you to call yourself Madame Duroc!" she said. She forced Hortense to marry the narcissist pervert brother of Napoléon, Louis Bonaparte. Yes, Hortense became Madame Bonaparte, but she suffered a great deal, and her marriage was a failure. She would have been much happier with Monsieur Duroc. Love never wins, I tell myself.

Wait—Duroc! What? I'm not supposed to be at Duroc station. Oh no! I'm going in the wrong direction. So stupid! Now I have to take the opposite line, but it's almost one o'clock in the morning, and the Métro will close soon.

I'm really like Cinderella now, running against the clock before my world turns back into a pumpkin. I dash out of the train and down the stairs to catch the last Métro.

Click-clack, click-clack, click-clack…

Chapter 2:

Tea with Coco Chanel

I'M SITTING AT ANGELINA'S, AN ELEGANT TEA ROOM NEXT TO the Louvre, with my American friend, Dorothy. As we wait for our order to arrive, we people-watch—especially the women. We are playing The Parisian Game, a game I invented. You have to guess who is a Parisienne, and who is not. In fact, Dorothy already knows how to recognize a Parisian woman because she's a photographer and has "the eye." She's a liberal, and a freelance photographer for prestigious American newspapers.

"She is, she is not, maybe she is—oh là là!" I say. "No, she is definitely not! Look at this woman! Her nails are too long. Her hair is too straight. Her breasts and lips are too big, and she wears too much makeup. Tight, white jeans with pearls? With white sneakers? Non! Plus, she's drinking Champagne at five o'clock. She is definitely not Parisian!"

"Not everyone can have a sober style as you," Dorothy says, smiling. "With your black dress, your pearls around your neck and wrists, and in your ears. You remind me of Coco Chanel."

"Thanks, my dear," I say. I take it as a compliment. Yes, indeed I'm a sober Parisian woman.

Dorothy is from Seattle and loves Paris. She would like to live in Paris while I (sometimes) would like to leave. She was intrigued by my many pictures of Coco Chanel on Facebook. We became Facebook friends first, then friends for real. Dorothy likes Chanel very much, too. Every time she comes to Paris, we have a tea at Angelina's.

"I can't agree more" says Dorothy, while she stares at the lady with her Champagne glass. "She's not Parisian, for sure. She must be in her twenties. I wonder where she comes from."

"We will know soon, my friend!" I answer with a mysterious smile. I jump up from my seat.

"You're not following her to the bathroom!" Dorothy laughs.

Several moments later, I return triumphant, and sit on the Louis XV armchair to relay the info: "So, the 'Too Much' woman is Russian." Indeed, I feel like a spy during the Cold War, my life, a John Le Carré fashion novel.

"I really don't understand young women," I say. "So obvious. I have a good Russian friend who is 40, and elegant. Nothing like with this young Russian woman."

"Maybe it's not a question of nationality but a question of generation?" Dorothy offers.

"It's a generational problem. Exactly! You're right. I've noticed that many young women are very artificial. They want to be sophisticated, but in fact, they are vulgar. As if they only want to please men, to be super sexy. I think the new aesthetic of the 21st century is 'I wanna be a porn star.' You know what Chanel used to say? 'Some people think luxury is the opposite of poverty. It is not. It is the opposite of vulgarity.' And believe me, nowadays, vulgarity is the new chic!"

"You're tough!" Dorothy looks serious as she savors her hot chocolate with cream, which seems delicious.

"Coco Chanel would be even worse than me," I say. "You should hear what she said about women who dared to show their knees. Plus, she said horrors about young women wearing trousers. I don't know who said Chanel was a feminist because she was not. Well, maybe she used to be when she was younger, but definitely not as she got older." I say. "You're right Dorothy. I'm not nice. But don't be too hard on me. I'm tough because Chanel's soul is talking to me right now." I say inhaling my refined Darjeeling tea.

From time to time, I have conversations with Coco Chanel at Angelina's because it was here that she used to have tea. She used to live at the very chic Hotel Ritz, which is close by. Coco had good taste.

I have a rule in life: never queue if you don't have to. Life is too short to queue. You'll never see me in Paris waiting for hours to enter a fancy restaurant, bar, or tearoom. Plus, I can't eat when people are waiting. I feel sorry for the crowd as they watch me, miserable, as I'm being seated at my table. That spoils all my joy of eating. The last time Parisians had to queue to eat was during the Second World War.

But I have one exception: Angelina's. Mister Ruppelmayer, who came from Austria, liked his daughter-in-law so much that he named his tearoom, "Angelina." Since 1903, all elegant women from Paris have come here to enjoy the best hot chocolate in the city. Because during the Belle Epoque, when you were an honorable Parisian woman, you could not go out on your own to a café or restaurant. You can do anything, now, of course, but then only prostitutes went out alone in public places. (French are not very modern, in case you didn't know already.) Guess when we had the right to vote here? In 1893, like the women from New Zealand? Not at all. In 1918, like our British sisters? No. In 1919, like our German sisters? Nein. In 1945. Even women from Uzbekistan had the right to vote before French women. France is a conservative country. I know many people won't agree, but I stand by what I say, and for me the best hot chocolate in Paris is Angelina's. They have a hot chocolate called l'Africain (the African) because it's made with three kinds of African chocolate beans (from Ghana, Nigeria, and the Ivory Coast). You can also add a pot of whipped cream. It's a rich chocolate, indeed.

The first time I went to Angelina's, I was 17 years old—meaning during the last century. Nothing has changed. The waiters are still charming women, wearing black aprons with white shirts. Angelina's is a Parisian institution. That's why so many people come here, because the tourists and the locals alike know they won't be disappointed. It's worth queuing for.

Angelina's, even for me, is a rite of passage. When my older son was also 17 years old, I invited him here. I told him, "You're a young man now, so you deserve the best hot chocolate in Paris—with their exclusive pastries." He was very impressed by the hot chocolate and amazed by the Mont Blanc pastry, made of chestnut cream and meringue. The problem is now he wants to go to Angelina's every weekend, but my budget doesn't allow for it. Angelina's is not cheap. But do you think that Mademoiselle Chanel used to have her tea in a cheap café of Paris? Of course not.

"I've been to Italy and London often for work," Dorothy says. "And I've noticed two things: The Italian woman is the epitome of femininity. Sophisticated with long hair, high heels, always groomed, and wearing bright colors. The British woman is more eccentric. She wears unique fashions and likes bold tights with interesting patterns. And the French woman, well…she wears only black. Why so much black?" she asks. "It's a bit sad, don't you think?" She buttons her pastel blue jacket up, which matches her pastel blue and white dress.

Dorothy reminds me of Shirley Temple, with her curly hair. But she would be a Rock and Roll Shirley Temple since she plays electric guitar. She even has five different guitars that she calls "her daughters." She is tall and athletic, thanks to the bicycle she fanatically rides every weekend near Mount Rainier, not far from Seattle. She's always enthusiastic about everything French. More enthusiastic than me. She has the soul of an artist.

"You are exaggerating, my dear." I reply with a mouthful of mille-feuille (my favorite Parisian pastry). "French women don't always wear black. Sometimes, they can be very eccentric, too, you know. They can wear navy blue or grey or even beige when they really want to be original." I smile. "Ok, I guess you are right. We like wearing black or dark colors.

I could tell you it's because it's easier; you don't take too many risks when you wear black. Maybe we are a bit too conventional, classic—and a little bit lazy, too. And black matches everything." I use a dramatic tone of voice and with my hand on my heart I say, "If we, the French women, wear so much black, it's because we are Chanel's daughters!"

"I like your answer!" Dorothy says. "Chanel was a talented woman. She still fascinates women of the world. Everybody, even my aunt, knows Chanel."

"Guess how many biographies of Coco have been written?" I say.

"I don't know…thirty?"

"Sixty! Every year, there is a new book about Chanel. Have you seen the queue of tourists in the Chanel shops? She still has a huge influence on fashion, for sure."

"She also freed women by eliminating the corset," adds Dorothy. "A torture tool for women. I'm glad we don't have to wear it."

"Actually, that is not really true about Chanel. It was another fashion designer, Paul Poiret, who decided to take away the corset, before Chanel, and it was in 1906. Can you imagine that woman used to wear painful corsets for four centuries? From the 16th to the 20th century."

"I can't even imagine. Thank you, Monsieur Poiret!" Dorothy says. "I saw Poiret clothes in Downtown Abbey, the television series. Then came the Roaring Twenties and a new fashion, The Boyish Style. La Garçonne, as you say in French."

"Et voilà!" I say. "Chanel's clothes became a hit. She arrived right on time. Karl Lagerfeld said Chanel invented everything except jeans. I never wear jeans because everybody wears jeans. It's boring wearing jeans. Wearing jeans is a lack of imagination. Well, to be honest, I'm also not skinny enough to wear jeans." I tell Dorothy, topping off her caloric hot chocolate with the very caloric whipped cream.

"Me either, I hardly wear jeans, now." says Dorothy. "Thanks to Paris."

"Paris? Why?"

"Before Paris, I never wore dresses. As you know I love bike riding. When I came to Paris, I saw all these Parisian women riding their bicycles in cute little dresses and high heels. You never see an American woman riding a bike in high heels. I really was impressed because Parisian women have style—even while bike-riding. So, I suddenly thought, 'Me, too! I want to be as stylish as a Parisian woman!' So, I bought a flower-print dress at H&M, hired a Vélib bicycle, and rode it from the Louvre to Notre Dame. For the first time in my life, I felt free and feminine. It was heaven!"

"I'm glad that Paris brought more style into your life. Style is more important than fashion. Even Chanel says so."

"It's not a coincidence that Chanel's daughters are so stylish," says Dorothy. "Style is everywhere in Paris. Even in bakeries the pastries are real masterpieces. And look at this place! I love Angelina—the glass ceiling, this table, these cups, and the teapots are all so elegant. Art of living is the religion of the French, and it has become mine, too. I'm newly converted!"

"Yes! Absolutely!" I say. "I call this phenomenon 'The ethic of the aesthetic.' French love aesthetes. The beauty in utility."

"And Paris deserves a little effort when getting dressed. It is worth it, to be elegant in Paris!"

"If I was the mayor of Paris, I would create the PFP."

"What's this? Dorothy asked, clearly misunderstanding my accent.

"The Paris Fashion Police, the P-F-P, and you would not be able to walk in Paris if you were wearing shorts and flip-flops. Or, you would have to pay a hefty fine."

"I like this program. I'm sure Paris would get a lot of money fining inelegant people."

Dorothy asks for the bill. She is a generous woman. Each time we see each other in Paris, she pays for me. Dorothy always says, "When I'm in Paris, I never count." Living in Paris when you are a single mom with two kids is a luxury. When tourists complain about Paris because it's an expensive city, I always reply, "I can't agree more, and imagine if you had to live here all year, like me!" Yes, living in Paris has a price. That's why I always have coffee at Paris cafés because it's the cheapest beverage. I never liked coffee because coffee is bitter in Paris. What I really like…is tea.

"Would you like to see the home of Miss Chanel?" I ask Dorothy as we leave Angelina's.

"Yes, of course"

"Ok, let's go see Coco."

• • •

After a ten-minute walk, we cross the magnificent Place Vendôme, passing Napoléon roosted on his column. Finally, we arrive at the beautiful entrance of the Hotel Ritz.

"Welcome to the Ritz," the concierge greets us with a big smile as we push open the revolving door of the palace. After Angelina and its Old-World ambiance, I'm still on a magical journey. The crystal lamps, the fluffy, wool carpet, the harp music, all come together to make me feel alive in a glamorous world. And there is the delightful perfume in the air. As soon as you arrive the scent of amber is in your head and your soul.

"This is luxury," I whisper to Dorothy. "The Hotel Ritz was the place where Coco Chanel lived, loved, and died. I'm like Coco. I want to live here!"

We walk in the most stylish way we can muster, in the direction of the corridor of the hotel, where there are plenty of comfortable, empty sofas waiting.

Dorothy asks as we sit, "Why didn't Coco live in the flat in her shop on Rue Cambon?"

"She was scared to be all alone in her big apartment at night. Don't forget, Chanel lived her entire life alone. She never married. Her business life was successful, but not her personal life."

"Yes, it's true. All her life, she was Mademoiselle Chanel, but she never became a wife. Well, it was not such a bad life after all." Dorothy gazes at the luxurious winter garden of the hotel.

"With all the tea I drank at Angelina, I really need to go to the toilet," I say. "I've heard that the Ritz's toilets are the most elegant in Paris, so I'm going to see if it's true."

A few minutes later, I returned, grinning.

"Indeed, the most elegant toilets of Paris. The faucets are golden swans. Incredible!"

"I wonder how much tea costs here?" Dorothy asks. "Let's go check."

With great confidence, we saunter in the direction of the tearoom. Inside the red and cozy place, there is a big painting of a man. He is pale with dark eyes and a little moustache. He's wearing a camellia on the lapel of an elegant jacket. "I know this man," I say. "It's Marcel Proust!"

"Thanks, Edith, but I recognized him," Dorothy says. "To me, Proust is the greatest French writer of the 20th century. I've noticed that the French know him, even if they haven't read all of 'In Search of Lost Time,' his masterpiece."

"I confess, I'm like those French," I say. "I've only read the first volume, 'Swann's Way.'" Suddenly, I'm struck by a thought. "Ah, of course!"

"Of course, what?" Dorothy asks.

"They put swans in the toilets because of Marcel Proust. What is the name of the hero, his double in Proust's novel? Charles Swann. You see, you can find literature even in the toilets of Paris!"

"Too funny." Dorothy chuckles. "But why did they put a portrait of Proust in the tearoom?"

"Because it's called the Marcel Proust Salon. Proust frequented the Ritz to find inspiration for his books. He always asked the concierge questions about the VIPs and aristocratic clients for his novel's characters," I explain. "He used to have dinner here and his favorite dessert was vanilla ice cream with gallons of coffee. You know, I had high tea here for free, once."

"Free? Really?"

"It was thirty years ago, and it was thanks to tea and poetry. It's a long story, so let's sit here. We have not tried these cute armchairs, yet. Once upon a time, in the late eighties…"

• • •

In the late '80s, you couldn't find decent tea in Parisian cafés. You could only hope for powdered tea in paper sachets served with lukewarm water that came in a stainless-steel teapot. Only the tearooms served tea worthy of the name. I always liked tea, so when I was 18 years old, I decided to do a solo tea pilgrimage to Darjeeling, India. Maybe you don't know, but Darjeeling tea is one of the most refined in the world. In those days, there was no internet, no fax, and no smartphone. And there were not many girls who traveled to India alone. A call from Calcutta—the biggest city next Darjeeling—to Paris? You'd better be rich. Back then, the only way to communicate with your family was via letters, which took at least one week to arrive.

I remember having tears in my eyes when I saw the tea fields of the prestigious Darjeeling tea in the Himalayas. I enjoyed India so much that I visited three times. People dream of honeymooning in Paris. Me, I did mine much later, in the Rajasthan province in India.

Anyway, after Darjeeling, I decided to go on my own to Yunnan, in China, to do another tea pilgrimage. Yunnan tea is an excellent black tea. Believe me, it really was an adventure to go to China alone in those days. I didn't speak a word of Chinese, and no one spoke a word of English. All the Chinese people wore the blue Mao suit. When I rode in a train, I was always the only Westerner, and the Chinese took pictures of me as if I was a Hollywood star. Everyone was so friendly. It was authentic China. I loved it so much that I also visited there three times.

For one of my birthday presents, my parents, who knew my passion for tea, helped me to join the prestigious Paris Tea Drinkers Club. I was very grateful to become an honorable member of this exclusive Parisian high society. We tasted excellent, delicate teas once a month in wondrous locales. One evening, we held our meeting in a cozy, exotic Chinese restaurant. During the dinner, the president of the club, a tea connoisseur and well-known writer, told us all:

"Dear members, as you know it's the Chinese New Year tonight and it's the year of the Rabbit. That's why I chose this restaurant for our meeting. I propose to honor this Chinese New Year by doing a poetry contest. Write a poem about a rabbit and tea. You have one hour."

Immediately, like all the other literary guests, I tried to write something about a rabbit and tea that rhymes, with my mouth full of Chinese noodles. Not so easy. One hour later, while we were eating delicious, warm and sweet cocoa balls served with a smoked Chinese Lapsang Souchong tea, the president announced the winner.

"My dear tea comrades, I have your poems, and all are excellent. It was very difficult to choose." Then he read the poem of the winner.

And among fifty refined, smart people, this prestigious writer had chosen...my poem!

The Pekinese Dog and the Girl Angora
Once upon a time,
In the land of the dragon king,
There was a girl Angora rabbit
In love with a Pekinese.
Alas, their love could not flower
Because the Angora rabbit
Drank only kava,
While the Pekinese
Liked only Chinese tea.
"If you love me, my sweet rabbit,"
Pled the Pekinese,
"You will drain the cup
Of this Oolong to the last drop!
The rabbit, crazed with love,
Drank the velvet-smooth infusion,
And thus, thanks to tea,
The two lovers were united for eternity."

Here is the original version in French, so you can hear the rhymes.

La lapine et le Pékinois

Il était une fois

Au pays du dragon roi

Une lapine angora

Qui était amoureuse d'un chien pékinois.

Hélas, Hélas, leur amour ne pouvait s'épanouir

Car la lapine angora

Ne buvait que du kawa

Alors que le petit chien pékinois

N'aimait que le thé chinois.

Si tu m'aimes ma douce lapine,

Implora le chien de Chine

Tu boiras jusqu'à la lie,

Le Oolong que voici!

La lapine folle d'amour

But le filtre de velours.

C'est ainsi que grâce au thé

Les deux amants furent réunis pour l'éternité.

If you aren't a tea lover, you probably don't know that Oolong tea is a Chinese black tea and that the dragon land is Bhutan, a little Buddhist kingdom in the Himalayas. I did not go to Bhutan (too expensive) but I went to Sikkim, another kingdom in the Himalayas.

I was very proud because in all my life, I'd never won an award. Even the award for the friendliest student at school I never won. And guess what the prize was for my poem? Tea for two at the Hotel Ritz.

A few days later, I was thrilled to have my high tea in the mystical Marcel Proust Tearoom. I'm like Marcel Proust; I love my mother. So, I decided to invite her to enjoy my memorable free tea for two at the chic Ritz.

• • •

My mother's name is Sarah, and she's had a tough life. Like my father, as a Jewish child, she had to be hidden from the Nazis during World War II, a Shoah survivor, as we call them now. At 6 years old, she had to memorize her new identity. She suddenly became "Suzanne" because in the 1940s, if your name was Sarah, you were automatically Jewish. She also had to learn Christian prayers, because she was hidden in a convent in Belgium–the country where she was born and raised. That's why I love nuns. They saved my mom's life. Later, she escaped to France.

Of course, my mother and father, like many Jews of Europe, lost family and friends. aunts, uncles, and among them, her Aunt Roiza; her Uncle Akiva Elbaum, and her beloved little cousins, Fanny and Marie, who were 10 and 12 years old. They were all arrested in France and deported to Auschwitz.

I never talk about the war with my parents because it's too pain-ful. For them and for me. My mother taught me three things: 1) Laugh at everything in life—even about the worst things; 2) Be a rebel; 3) Love history and French literature. When she was 18 years old, in the late '50s, against the will of her parents, she moved to Israel on her own, to the north of the country, in Galilee, and built a very left wing, francophone Kibbutz. She also did her military service, of course. Thanks to Emile Zola, she met my father there. Both my parents worshipped Zola, a brilliant and coura-geous French writer.

Then, my sister was born. But my mother couldn't bear this austere community life anymore. "I knew this life was not for me when we all had to vote to choose the color of my bedroom curtains," she told me. "I told your father, 'Let's go back to Paris and its civilized cafés.'"

So, the family returned to civilization, and I was born in Belleville, a working-class neighborhood in northern Paris.

• • •

"It's here, exactly where you're sitting, that Mademoiselle Chanel used to have her tea," the waitress of the Ritz tearoom, who looked like a Chanel model, told my mother and I as we prepared to enjoy our free high tea.

"Impressive!" My mother said, as she and I were seated on a black-and-white velvet sofa, surrounded by delicious pastries.

The Darjeeling tea was perfect. Everything is always perfect at the Ritz. I got the attention of the stylish waitress and asked, "Do you think it would be possible to visit Chanel's bedroom, Mademoiselle?"

She said it was not possible. "It's reserved for clients of the hotel."

My mother whispered to me, "And do you think that Mademoiselle Chanel took her tea with her lover, the Nazi officer von Dincklage?" She put a madeleine cake in her mouth all at once.

"Well, I guess." I replied. "But it's also here where she was arrested for 'collaboration with the enemy' after WWII. She was set free, so I guess she was not a Nazi, after all."

"Or, she had connections," my mother said with a dark look. "Do you know what she did during the war? There was a French law called The Aryan Law, which forbade Jews from owning businesses in France." She explained that before the Second World War, Chanel sold her perfume, Number 5, to the Wertheimer brothers, who were French Jews. She couldn't imagine that her perfume would be such a hit. She became very angry with the new owners and asked them to give back her perfume brand. They refused, so in 1942 she told the French administration, "The Wertheimer brothers are Jewish, therefore they are not allowed to own my perfume." Since she wasn't Jewish, she argued that she should be able to get it back from them. But too bad for her, the brothers passed the ownership to a French Catholic friend while they were in the process of escaping to the U.S.

"What do you think of that, my daughter?" my mother asked. "And why did she have a code name during the war if she wasn't a spy for the Germans?"

I debated that it was because she went to Madrid, and Spain at that time was Fascist, allied with Germany, and she needed authorization from the French administration as well as a visa to visit there. "She was friends with the English and the Germans so she thought she could make peace in Europe." She was traumatized by the millions of casualties during the First World War. Chanel wanted her good friend, Churchill, whom she met in Spain, and the Germans, to end the war. "Maybe she was anti-Semitic, like many French back then, but don't forget she was coming from a little village and had no education and many prejudices."

I said that I thought Coco Chanel was being very naïve, and maybe a little pretentious, to think that she could make the peace just because her name was Chanel, but I didn't think she was a spy for the Nazis. She was patriotic, and closed her shop during the war when many French did not. And after the war, she reconciled with the Wertheimer brothers, negotiating a new deal with them.

"She was not a friendly woman, I agree," I said, "and she would have refused to be my friend, for sure, but it's not a crime."

"Bravo! You could have been her lawyer." My mother smiled. "You know what? My dear daughter, it's always useful in life to have a powerful Englishman who has a crush on you. Without Churchill, who gave the order to set Chanel free, nobody would know who Chanel is now. There wouldn't be a Chanel suite at the Ritz. Thank you, Winston!" my mother exclaimed, while sipping her refined English tea.

"Mummy, I admire Chanel even if I don't like her," I said. "She wasn't a nice person, but she was a genius, and the first female entrepreneur of France."

André Malraux, the Minister of Culture once said of Chanel, "In France, the 20th century will remember three names: de Gaulle, Picasso, and Chanel." Not bad.

"Et voilà, Dorothy. This is how I won my tea for two at the Ritz."

"I'm impressed."

I thank her. "Alright, so now let's get out of here or we'll stay all day long. It's so chic here. J'adore le Ritz."

As we exit the Ritz hotel, I'm admiring the iron balcony of La Place Vendôme. Each time I'm in this magnificent place, I can't help but think about Coco Chanel. She used to cross the same square each evening to go to her bedroom in the hotel. I'm sure that, like me, she was not too tired to admire this incredible royal square. I can see the golden symbols on the mansion's facades. The golden human faces with rays of sunshine. They look like a sun, and they're all around the square. It reminds of the medallions with sunshine rays at Versailles, the symbol of the Sun King, Louis the XIVth, because this square was built under his reign. It's Apollo, the Greek God of sun, music and arts, the symbol of the French king.

Mademoiselle Chanel was a kind of Sun Queen in her own way. The queen of the black and white, the empress of French fashion, the guru of good taste. Exactly like Louis the XIVth used to be. Louis the XIVth admired classic Greek aesthetics. Nothing overly ornate like the Italians created in the Baroque period. The elegant buildings lining the Place Vendôme are exactly the illustration of the motto of Louis the XIVth: Symmetry, Balance, and Harmony.

Classic architecture, exactly like the palace of Versailles. Chanel was also classic in her fashion. And the French women are still classic, too. I remember reading a quote on Chanel in Vogue once. She said something like, 'Fashion is not something in dresses only. Fashion is in the sky, in the street, fashion has to do with ideas, the way we live. Fashion is architecture."

Parisian style is in the Parisian streets. Chanel, like the other Parisian women, was inspired by the architecture of Paris.

We walk a few minutes along the chic rue du Faubourg Saint-Honoré, where the most refined fashion brands live, and we arrive in Rue Cambon, in front of the legendary Chanel boutique.

I want to open the heavy door of the prestigious shop but an impressive security guard beats me to it. Just on the right of the entrance, inside the shop, there is a large photograph of Coco in her thirties. Next to the huge portrait, we could also glimpse the famous staircase.

"Look!" I point out the majestic white stairs. "This is where Coco used to sit during her fashion shows. Her apartment was upstairs."

We enter the fashion mecca. Dorothy and I are giddy like teenagers. The clients, mostly Asians, are well-dressed and soft-spoken. The entire Chanel staff is very polite and friendly. The stylish salespeople wear black dresses and fresh makeup. They all smile warmly, "Bonjour Madame." It's magical. We feel like VIPs.

Dorothy and I admire the mirrors, paintings, white candles, the shoes, and the Chanel accessories. Dorothy's eyes sparkle at the spectacle of outfits dancing on their hangers. I caress the fabrics: the cashmere of the coats, the silk of the dresses, the linen of the trousers, the satin shirts, the wool jackets. I can feel Chanel's soul. The spirit of Coco is everywhere in this place, both in the refined interior design and in the clothes. Of course, everything smells of Chanel No. 5, "a perfume that smells like a woman" as Coco used to say. Everything is simple and luxurious.

After one hour of being in the world of elegance, we decide to leave. We have to tear ourselves away.

Outside, it has started to rain. I complain.

"You call this rain?" Dorothy from Seattle says. "This is nothing. Where I come from, it rains almost every day. Who cares about the rain when you're in Paris!"

"I guess you're right. Let's go! Follow me!"

In the rain, we run as fast as we can in our dresses and high heels. We find a small church and trot up the stairs to the entry.

"It's lovely here, so intimate," says Dorothy, looking up at the cupola. She attempts to dry her hair with her blue scarf.

"And dry," I say. "Let's sit on these chairs. Here was the last mass for Coco's best friend, Misia Sert. She was Polish, and this is a Polish church."

"Chanel had a temper, so I guess her friend was no shrinking violet, either."

"You bet! Chanel is like a Russian doll. You open the doll, and you find incredible people in and all around her."

I'm fascinated by Misia Sert, it's a shame she's not well known because she was a genius in her own right. She was the muse of great painters from the Belle Epoque, like Toulouse-Lautrec, Renoir, Vuillard, and Bonnard. She was also the muse of musicians. Her piano teacher was the renowned French composer, Gabriel Fauré. She was so talented that he cried when he learned she would not become a professional pianist. And Maurice Ravel, one of my favorite composers, used to seek her advice about his music. Le Boléro by Ravel is the most-aired song in the world. A few years ago, there was an incredible exhibition at Musée d'Orsay called Misia, Queen of Paris. I always wondered how a woman like Chanel, who knew nothing about art, music, and literature, became best friends with Picasso, or Cocteau? Or Diaghilev, the PR agent of the famous Russian ballet. How did she become the lover of the French poet, Reverdy? And why did Stravinsky, not the worst Russian composer, fall in love with her? An uneducated orphan from nowhere learned how to mingle with these rich and chic Bohemians. Talk about how to be well-read and impress the rich and the famous in ten lessons. Her best friend, Misia Sert, was her coach. Chanel could not belong to high society because she was perceived as just a seamstress for duchesses. Would you invite the Pizza Hut delivery boy to your fancy parties? Of course not. But before Misia, there is also her English lover. I don't mean, the Duke of Westminster. The English Duke came later. I'm talking about Boy. That was his nickname. He was the one who came from high society and taught her good manners. Chanel has said that Boy was everything to her: her lover, her family, and her best friend. He was refined, educated, and wore the chicest clothes that she herself copied. He looked like Freddie Mercury, the singer of the band Queen. Lucky woman to have such a great lover. Yeah. He was so great that he married someone else, a young Englishwoman from the English upper crust. Misia arrived in Chanel's life just after Boy died in a car accident. Misia Sert had refinement, education, taste, and most importantly, she knew the right people. She was Chanel's key to open the formerly closed rich, snobbish world of Paris. Thanks to Misia, Chanel rubbed shoulders with VIPs, filled up her address book and order book with the Who's Who, and became herself fashionable, success-ful, and rich. Of course, Chanel was very talented but without Misia, it would have been a slow and difficult road to success. Sometimes someone or something is your key to a new world. The main reason I admire Chanel is because she went from the orphanage to the Ritz! Not bad, huh?

I point toward the church's door. "Listen."

"I hear nothing."

"Exactly. Because it stopped raining. We can leave now."

As we walk along the Tuileries Garden, we inhale the sweet aroma of the newly moistened grass.

Dorothy thanks me for taking her into Chanel. "I wouldn't have had the courage to go alone," she says. "Sometimes, I'm shy and intimidated by Paris, and by the Parisians. From time to time, I feel like I'm still a little girl from small town America. From nowhere."

I remind her that Chanel also came from nowhere. "Because of that she wasn't weighed down by a traditional French family and their conser-vative values. She was free, so she was modern."

In the Belle Époque, the other stylish designers had to train for years in the famous fashion studios of Paris before opening their own fashion boutiques. Not Chanel. She opened her own hat shop straight away in 1909, then her fashion shop—without any training. When you are unen-cumbered by the weight of tradition, a family with a long history, the con-servative notions of schooling, it's easier to reinvent yourself.

"What you think is your weakness can be your strength," I tell Dorothy. "Chanel decided to escape from her environment, follow her pas-sion. She was not afraid, and she succeeded. Following your passion with-out asking yourself too many questions. That's the key to success."

"You know what?" Dorothy says, "I'm just realizing that I followed the exact same path as Chanel!" Then Dorothy told me how she also escaped from her narrow-minded environment. She was from a small town in Washington state and always felt different from her family and friends. She wasn't an orphan, fortunately, and her parents were good to her, but she wanted to escape from a boring town and boring life.

For her 18th birthday, Dorothy got a subscription to Vogue. Each month, this fashion magazine was like oxygen to her. Suddenly, she had access to a sophisticated world she hadn't known before: refined women, an elegant way of life, a place where art was important. Something far from her American rural life.

"I knew I wanted to belong to this creative world," Dorothy says. "I discovered fashion but more importantly, I discovered the pictures of fashion. Photography became my passion."

"Who said fashion is superficial?" I ask her. "How did you follow your passion?"

"First, I took photography classes in Seattle. But Paris was my second passion. Vogue introduced me to Paris because there were so many photos of models wearing French fashions set in the magnificent streets of Paris. But I couldn't afford to visit Paris. My parents weren't rich, and they were already paying my rent in Seattle while I worked as a waitress to pay for my photography classes." While she couldn't travel to Paris, she could see Paris, admiring the City of Light through the eyes of French photographers: Parisian kids playing in the streets captured by Robert Doisneau, Paris at night thanks to Brassaï, and nostalgic, lost Paris by Eugène Atget.

Not being able to see Paris for real, opened the door of a new world to her. Her imagination compensated for her frustration.

"I had to find another way to see and learn about Paris. So, I found a tool to feed my passion—the artistic tool. All these French photographers became my guide to Paris. They were, and still are, my mentors."

"So, your key was not a woman or a lover like Coco Chanel, but a magazine. Vogue was your key to a different and artistic universe."

"Absolutely. Vogue changed my life."

"Your passion for Paris reminds me of a love story. It's like you were falling in love with a man you would never meet. But what happened when you saw Paris for the first time? Because, once, I fell in love with a man I met on the internet, and when I met him in person, it was a huge disappointment. I cried a lot."

"Fortunately, I didn't cry, but my first time in Paris was a shock—but in a good way. I realized that Paris was the city for artists, outcast people, like me. Later, I did my best to come to Paris twice a year for ten years, thanks to my residual income. Little by little, I understood that I could be myself in Paris, instead of the charade I was playing in the States. I knew deep down that my home was Paris. Of course, I wanted to live here, like my French idols—those French photographers—but it seemed like a fantasy."

"I've met so many foreigners who would like to live in Paris. But when you don't master the language or the culture, or you have no friends, family, or a decent job, Paris can be really hard, believe me."

"I was very depressed, stuck in my foggy city, dreaming about Paris. Then one day, I decided to stop dreaming and do something about it. It took me many years to make it happen. I studied French long distance from Seattle to understand more about Paris. I watched all of the classic black-and white-films of Truffaut and Godard, in French with English subtitles."

"Well done!" I say. "François Truffaut is my favorite director, you know. He's so sensitive. He really loved French women."

"And I listened to the Parisian singers from the sixties," she said. "Juliette Greco, Jeanne Moreau, and Barbara. I sang their songs in my basement with my guitar when I had insomnia."

"You have good taste," I offer. "These amazing Parisian women are my icons, too. Maybe we should do a duo because, with my name, Edith, everybody must think I'm a talented singer." I laugh.

"And now—" Dorothy takes a deep breath. With a voice choked with emotion she says, "You are the first one I am telling this to. In a few months, if things work out, I'm moving to Paris for good!"

"Dorothy, it's fantastic! I'm so happy for you!" I say. "I really admire you. You're very courageous because you did all this by yourself. Like

Chanel. A self-made woman. You are the living example that following your passion can change your life."

"Let's celebrate!" Dorothy says. She invites me for a glass of wine on a café terrace.

"It's very nice of you, Dorothy, but I don't like wine," I admit.

"What? How can you be French and not like wine? That's not very French."

"Damn it! You've found me out," I say. "I'm not French! I confess, I'm a spy." I laugh. "I know, it's weird. Well, the only wine I like is Champagne. Does that qualify me enough to be French?"

She nods. "I invite you for a glass of Champagne then."

"It's a bit early for Champagne but let's do it! And as Coco Chanel said, 'I only drink Champagne on two occasions: when I'm in love and when I'm not'."

"So, let's do as Coco says." Dorothy winks "Because I'm in love…with Paris!"

Chapter 3:

Flirting with Hemingway

EVERY TIME I ASK AN AMERICAN LIVING IN PARIS, "WHAT DO you do for a living?" he answers, "I'm a writer." Then, when I make polite small talk with the American writer about his wonderful life in Paris, I quickly realize that he is not a writer at all. He is a tour guide or English teacher in Paris, or an accountant for some American firm.

All very honorable professions, but I guess it's more romantic to introduce yourself as a writer than an accountant, especially when you want to impress a woman. However, not all women react the same way. Ted, an American expatriate, explained to me that he is very successful with French ladies as soon as he says he is a writer. French women are immediately interested in him and ask many questions, which boosts his ego. "Oh, how fascinating! And what do you write?"

But when he returns home to California, the American women turn their backs on him because as he says, "for American women, being a writer means being poor."

It's true that the French love art and worship artists. For us, art is more important than money, almost always.

I have noticed that since Woody Allen's movie "Midnight in Paris," there are more and more American writers in Paris. If you haven't already seen this popular film, I'll sum it up: an American writer arrives in Paris and is transported back to the 1920s where he meets his idol, Ernest Hemingway. By the way, ask any Parisian if he or she liked "Midnight in Paris" and you'll get a shrug. "Not at all. The movie is full of clichés about Paris" I've met so many Americans who pretend to be writers in Paris, that I now call this phenomenon, "The Hemingway Syndrome." Like his icon, Ernest Hemingway, this American writer is looking for inspiration in charming Parisian cafés. He writes his literary masterpiece while sipping a café crème, and late into the night, has intellectual discussions, sipping a cheap but excellent wine in a cheap but good restaurant. In France, wine is cheaper than a diet Coke. I know this because I prefer to drink Diet Coke.

We all know the famous Hemingway quote from his early days in Paris writing his novel, A Movable Feast: "Paris was always worth it and you received return for whatever you brought to it. But this is how Paris was in the early days when we were very poor and very happy." Yes, they ate well and cheaply, and drank well and cheaply, and they were happy in Paris.

With the passing years, I have also noticed that the American writer in Paris is not always a man but often a woman. And that's great. After all, why can't a woman do the same thing as a man?

When I ask the American writer in Paris what he is writing about, he answers: "I write about Paris. I fell in love with Paris, felt at home. I'm sure I used to be Parisian in another life, it's incredible."

Yeah. Incredible, indeed. Don't get me wrong, I perfectly understand that you can fall in love with Paris. Me too. I'm in love with my city. It's just that if you were hearing like me, hundreds of times, "I fell in love with Paris," you would be a little bit blasé, too. I met so many American writers in Paris that I'm seriously wondering if America doesn't have more writers than readers. Do you know how many books are written in English about Paris? This goes on for 101 pages on Amazon! There are 101 pages of Paris book titles. Twenty percent are French books translated into English, but eighty percent are written by Anglophones (among them a majority written by Americans).

If you are a Paris lover, your passion will be satisfied, because there is a lot of choice: You have the secret, new, hidden, underground, lost, waking up, revealed, inside and decorated Paris. Then there is barefoot in Paris, running barefoot in Paris, Paris like a local, and not-like-a-tourist Paris. If you are a literary person, help yourself: there's literary Paris, Paris by books, Romanticism in Paris, the little bookshop of Paris, the Paris library, The Paris librarian, Paris in mind, and the writers in Paris.

Then you have the food—yummy! The food's lover in Paris, the delicious days in Paris, a taste of Paris, hungry for Paris, bread and books in Paris, the Paris cheese shop, my Paris kitchen. A dessert? The sweet life in Paris, Paris sweets, the pastry shop of Paris, pancakes in Paris, the chocolate shop of Paris, the loveliest chocolate shop in Paris, the little Paris patisserie, the little bakery of Paris and the bakers of Paris. But maybe you would prefer a breakfast in Paris, a lunch in Paris, teatime in Paris, or dining out in Paris? And if there is sunshine, what could be better than a Paris picnic, a Paris picnic club, or maybe just between meals in Paris.

If you ate too much food, walking is always a good idea. So, let's walk in Paris and let's admire: the buildings, the doorways, the rooftops, the mansions, the balconies, a corner, l'appart, the only street, the air and even the mountains of Paris …et oui!

Sometimes the American writer just needs a year, a winter, April, a season, a summer, Sundays, a Christmas, the night before Christmas, a long night, a month, three weeks or only moments in Paris to write his book about Paris. If you like to be scared in Paris don't worry, there are plenty of dark serial killers in the City of Light. You'll read about the crimes of Paris, the crime beat in Paris, little crimes of Paris, a crime suspense in Paris, a true tale of crime in Paris, murder in Paris, story of a murder in Paris, Paris from murders, death in Paris, Paris in the dark, Paris vendetta, poison in Paris, twilight in Paris, all the devils in Paris, a Paris mystery, the Paris detective and at last a shadow in Paris. Cherchez la femme? There are many women in Paris: An American woman in Paris, an American girl in Paris, the lost girls of Paris, girl missing in Paris, the Paris party girl, the Paris wife, the mistress of Paris and the seamstress Paris,

Then you have the American, British or Australian love story in Paris. Ah! L'amour! Love from Paris, love in Paris, from Paris with love, Paris in love, the love letters to Paris, and falling in love in the City of Light. What else? If you are more conservative you can read first the honeymoon in Paris, then the wedding in Paris and, alas, le divorce in Paris.

I have not yet found "Le ménage à trois in Paris." So, if you are looking for a new angle for your book about Paris, I'm glad to help! Fortunately you don't need to be rich and only buying a piece of Paris or be homeless in Paris is enough to write your book about Paris. You don't have to be a human being either because American cat and expat dog are able to write their books about Paris too. But even Paris has an end my friend, so the American writer in Paris will say, "goodbye Paris," "I'll see you in Paris" or will advise you to "see Paris before you die." But please don't cry because fortunately, you and I, "We'll always have Paris." Well, you more than me because I'm a little bit tired of Paris.

Do you want more? Really? After reading 101 pages of Paris books, I confess I had a headache and became sick of Paris. An American woman (who wrote a book about a famous Parisian woman) told me: "You should be positive, because if there are so many books written by Americans about Paris it's because we love you!"

Yeah. They love me. I'm sure all these Anglophone books are great. I just have a little lingering question: is it true love—or just marketing? I'm looking for a book whose title would be, "I Have Never Been to Paris, but I Wrote My Book About Paris Because I Have to Pay the Bills." Just put the word Paris in the title and you'll sell well because Americans have a huge fantasy about this city. As Reg Crowder, an American friend of mine who lives in France told me (and who is writing a book about his life in France, per my advice), "You can't blame them. They're just trying to make money so they can come back to Paris." He's right. Living in Paris, even just for a day, is wonderful.

But I'm wondering something: If Americans like Paris so much, why don't they read books written by Parisians about Paris? Most of the Paris books written in French are translated into English. That's the good thing about globalization. If, like me, you're a fan of thrillers, you should read Léo Mallet who, way back in the '50s, had the brilliant idea to set a murder in each arrondissement of Paris. His detective, Nestor Burma, is so popular in France that there is a TV series based on his books.

You like the Roaring Twenties and Midnight in Paris? Then read Dan Franck and his wonderful book "Boheme" (you can find it in English). Same about our wonderful literature and history. Read the French, too. Try Baudelaire, who invented the concept of the flâneur (the stroller) or Zola, Hugo, Proust, and Balzac who are the real Paris experts.

If you are not a fan of French classic literature, there are hundreds of modern, smart, funny French authors who wrote also about food, architecture, and romance in the City of Light. There is even a book about where to pee in Paris.

You know what? I would love to talk more about the many books written in English about Paris. But right now, I'm a bit busy. Terribly sorry, but I must leave you, my dear, because…I have a book about Paris to write.

Yes, I too confess that I have the Hemingway Syndrome. I can even tell you where and how I caught this disease. Of course, I knew Hemingway for a long time. All French kids study "The Old Man and the Sea." For me, Hemingway was a bit like Victor Hugo, a classic writer, old and wise, with a white beard.

Then I met Björn, who was neither old nor had a white beard. I was in an Irish youth hostel as a student. I love Ireland. It's one of my favorite countries in Europe, even if it rains almost every day. Björn was a Swedish physics student and he invited me to visit his home in the south of Sweden, in Malmö. I fell in love with the kanelbullar there, delightful Swedish cinnamon buns. Then when Björn came to visit me in Paris, it was love at first sight for him and the Parisian croissant.

I was deeply in love with him. He used to call me "my passionate French lover." I never considered myself as a passionate woman, but maybe compared to Swedes I am. One evening, while we were crossing the Seine with the moonlight behind us, he told me, "I have one passion in life." Of course, I thought this passion was me. I whispered to him with a sweet voice, "Who is your passion?"

His answer: "Nuclear physics."

This is how our love story ended. The Swedish nuclear physicist destroyed our French romance. But Björn became a good friend, and it was he who helped me discover Hemingway in Paris. He advised me to read "A Movable Feast," and said it was a love poem between a writer and Paris. And he was right. I read it in French, of course. Hemingway has a real talent for making you feel his passion for Paris. So, I started to like him very much (Hemingway, not Björn). I read a book about his life to learn more about him. And I discovered that Hemingway is a legend. He looks like the hero of his novels: he weighed 220 pounds, was the clone of the seductive Clark Gable. He liked fishing and hunting. He was a man who had known three wars, four wives, who loved nature, literature, Cuba, and of course, Paris. He's also an author who fascinated women and who still fascinates men, mostly American men. He was also JFK's favorite author.

But really, Hemingway is a legend. Everybody can identify with him because he has many sides: a gentleman, a committed writer, a revolutionary writer, a virile adventurer who worshipped books, alcohol, and women. Hundreds of books have been written about Ernest—his life, his prose, his women, and even his subconscious. As his good friend Marlene Dietrich said, "What is most incredible about Ernest is that he found time to do what most men only dream of."

Hemingway is probably the most well-known American expatriate in the world. This charismatic writer still interests Americans. Every year, at least two new books are published about his life or his work. Theses and articles are devoted to him. There is even "The Hemingway Review" which is published in Idaho where he died, which offers articles about Hemingway twice a year. Who can resist him? Certainly not me.

So, when Le Bar Hemingway at the Hotel Ritz was finally reopened after three and a half years' renovation, of course, I wanted to go. But I couldn't find a friend to go with me. They were all too busy. I was tired of waiting, so I decided to go on my own. But I never go to bars because I don't like drinking alcohol, so going on my own was a big challenge. I'm a bit shy, so I was afraid to go at night by myself. A woman? Alone? At night? In a bar? What will people think? Am I looking for a little something-something? Naughty girl! But my love for Hemingway was stronger than my timidity so, one evening, I went. Alone. I brought a book with me because I was worried about feeling lonely and bored in this iconic place.

And there I was. I perched myself as comfortably as I could on a bar-stool and read my book. But after a short spell, I put my book down on the red mahogany bar because, in fact, it's impossible to read in this bar. The light is so dim that the only thing I can read is the cocktail menu. No problem. I, of course, choose the Hemingway cocktail. Don't ask me what's in it. I have no idea. The only thing I can tell is that there's some pretty strong alcohol in there, for sure, because it's a powerful cocktail. It's sweet and acid at the same time, exactly like Ernest.

I wondered if Hemingway used to drink this glamorous beverage when he came to liberate the Hotel Ritz during World War II. I also wondered why there are two bars in the Ritz. Ah, oui! Because one was reserved for women and one for men only. But one Saturday evening in the 1920s, at midnight, an unknown French girl wanted to have fun. So, she decided to have a cocktail in this small place with Hemingway, Fitzgerald, and Cole Porter.

"Let's do it! Let's fall in love," I hear Cole Porter singing. I hear, also, the crushing of ice, and see the barman, all in white, shaking my drink energetically. I hear the elegant people next to me speaking in English, softly. There is a sepia glow from the lights; I feel like I'm in the Roaring Twenties—it's amazing! The mood is pure magic.

I drank my cocktail like lemonade, so my brain is foggy now. I can feel a man staring at me; for sure he has a crush. Perched on my stool, I check my purple lipstick with my pocket mirror, and cross my legs to allure. The man is seductive but intimidating. I blush. He must be in his late fifties, a robust man, with a mustache. He doesn't smile, but his look is ironic.

It's Hemingway. There are plenty of Hemingway's pictures in this tiny bar.

How many times did he come to Paris? Seven: 1921, 1929, 1933, 1934, 1937, 1944, and for the last time in 1956. I have goosebumps just thinking that Hemingway was exactly where I am.

His last time in Paris was the most important because he found his treasure chest, which had been sleeping in the Ritz's basement for many years. In a forgotten suitcase were his notebooks, written in 1928, all his notes from when he was a young man in Paris. And what did he do with these notebooks he found thirty years later? He wrote "A Movable Feast"— the last book about his life. Hemingway's last literary work was about Paris.

Then he committed suicide. And this love poem for Paris was only published in 1964, three years after Ernest shot himself. Sad.

I suddenly have an inspired idea: to create a Hemingway tour for American tourists in Paris. I'm sure I'll be very successful.

"Yes, of course! A guided visit about me—again!" Hemingway is looking at me with his ironic look.

Pfffff. I sigh, and I shrug my shoulders. Alright, it's not really an original idea, I admit to the black-and-white rendition of Hemingway on the wall. All American tour guides in Paris propose an "In the footsteps of Hemingway" tour. Who am I, anyway, to dare being the Hemingway expert in Paris? I'm not even American. I'm not even Anglophone. "I know nothing about American literature," I tell Ernest on the wall, "and I've never read your books in English. Ok, I give up. You're right. It was stupid and pedantic. I'm sorry."

Hemingway stares me down. "You give up? After five minutes? What a brave woman you are. I'm really impressed."

"Very funny," I say. "It's easy for you. You can't imagine how impressive you are! I don't have a Nobel Prize in literature. I am Madame Nobody. I have zero legitimacy to do a tour about you. So, oui, I give up!" I don't want to be ridiculous.

"Sorry 'Madame Nobody,'" says the Hemingway in my head. "I didn't mean to be rude. You know that I do like women. Don't give up. What do you have that the American guides in Paris don't have?"

I had no idea. "I have zero knowledge about your books, your life, or your work. I know almost nothing about your life after Paris. Plus, last time I studied English, I was 12 years old. Yeah, right, fantastic idea. Merci." I needed another cocktail to cheer me up.

"Wait a minute, young lady," Hemingway shames me, "you were born, raised, educated, and married in Paris. No?"

"You can also add divorced."

"Only once? Oh, please, you're just a baby. I had four wives. Maybe you're not a Hemingway expert, but you're a true Parisienne. You know about Paris, and French culture."

So, a Hemingway tour through the eyes of a native Parisian? This Hemingway fella is right.

"Yeah! You got it!" Hemingway cheers me on. "What have you got to lose? Go get 'em!"

• • •

With "A Movable Feast" in my purse, I'm ready to look for the real life of Hemingway in Paris. I'm where he used to live when he arrived in Paris with Hadley, his first wife: 74 Rue Cardinal Lemoine. I glance up at the third floor of Ernest's building. There's a plaque in his honor written in French.

This district used to be a working-class neighborhood without running water. I grab the book and read the description of his apartment: "a two-room flat that had no hot water and no inside toilet facilities except for a bucket." I really admire Hadley. I don't think I would have followed a man to a place where you had a bucket for a toilet, even if that place is Paris.

Ernest and Hadley arrived in Paris December 21, 1921. Hemingway complained about the weather. "Then there was the bad weather" is even the first sentence of his book.

Paris still has bad weather in December. I'm freezing. I really need a good coffee. Where to go? I know! I'll find the "good café" in Place Saint-Michel that appears in Chapter One of A Moveable Feast! I'll just follow the path of Hemingway.

I jog along next to Saint Etienne du Mont church and find the windy Place du Panthéon. The Panthéon is the place where all the great French men are buried: Voltaire, Rousseau, Zola, and Hugo. I read an inscription on the façade: Aux grands hommes, la patrie reconnaissante—To the Great Men from a Grateful Homeland.

By the way, what about the great women? History is always written by men, about men. When will we talk about the great French women?

Next to the Panthéon there is another Neoclassical building. I have to stop because I'm moved. Like Hemingway, I suddenly remember my own youth in Paris when I was a young and naïve girl. This elegant building is the Panthéon-Sorbonne, the law section of La Sorbonne University. This is my university. I remember how impressed I was when I arrived as an 18-year-old in this mythical place that has existed since 1253. I studied French law for five years here, where I learned to be an educated woman, and a citizen.

While I'm waxing nostalgic about the good old days, I arrive at Place Saint Michel. I couldn't find the "good café on the Place St-Michel" that Hemingway wrote about in "A Movable Feast," the café where he used to write about Michigan while he was drinking café au lait. There seems like hundreds of cafés around this square, so I choose Café Fénelon, a discreet, locals-only place. I'm sure Ernest would approve of my choice.

It's too cold to sit outside with a view of the archangel Saint Michael killing the dragon in the big fountain. I sit inside on a comfortable mole-skin couch and, like Ernest did almost one hundred years ago, order a café au lait.

"Why is this café's name Fénelon?" I hear Hemingway ask. "I'm sure there's a Rue Fénelon not far from here."

"Nope, Ernest. It's because of Lycée Fénelon, which is located behind this café. It's the first high school created for girls only, in 1892." Fénelon was an intellectual and a priest who wrote a book in the 17th century promoting the education of girls. It's still a very prestigious high school. Lycée Fénelon is in the top ten schools in France for literature. "My sister used to study there," I say, "because she was a top student. She could read books in Latin! Can you imagine? Not like me."

"This Mister Fénelon was right!" Hemingway says. "I do like educated women."

"Not so macho after all, Monsieur Hemingway. I guessed that you like educated women. Your teacher in Paris was also an educated woman: Gertrude Stein. An educated woman, who was also a lesbian and old enough to be your mother."

"It's true, thanks to her I discovered painters who were not so well known in the 1920s: Matisse, Soutine, Picasso, Juan Gris, Braque, and Cézanne. I discovered Cubism in her literary salon while we were drinking tea and eating cookies. I remember it was next to Luxembourg Garden, not far from where we are now. Le Jardin du Luxembourg is my favorite garden in Paris."

"You know what I think?" I say, "Gertrude taught you how to write. Simple language and straightforward prose. And a musical repetition of words. 'A rose is a rose is a rose,' she said. This writing style was very modern and new at the time."

"Maybe," Hemingway says. "It's also Mrs. Stein who told me to quit my job as a journalist and dedicate myself to writing. I guess she wasn't such a bad teacher after all. Even if she was a little arrogant."

"Oh, and you're not? What about your image: macho-man writer, world traveler, adventurer—and womanizer?"

I hear Ernest laugh, loud and heartily. "An insolent Parisian woman you are!"

I tell him that I'm French, and the French are outspoken. "You know, all my girlfriends hate you. They say you're a cheater, a chauvinist, an egomaniacal narcissist-alcoholic. I even have a friend who does a tour in Paris about your four wives because she hates you and wants everyone to know why."

"Charming."

"But Gertrude wrote that you were extraordinarily handsome and charismatic, and I couldn't agree more. Even with all your flaws, I still like you."

"Thanks, darling!"

"In this politically correct society where smoking a cigar in a café is a crime, we need charismatic, subversive, and flamboyant writers like you. It's funny."

"What's funny, darling?"

"You wrote about Michigan when you were in Paris," I muse, "and Paris when you were in the States. You wrote "A Movable Feast" in Idaho, right?"

"Maybe away from Paris I could write about Paris, and in Paris I could write about Michigan." Hemingway quotes Chapter One to me: "Sometimes you need to be far away from your homeland to have inspiration."

I tell him that I see what he's getting at. "That's why there were so many American writers in Paris in the Twenties. Far away from your home, you feel more at home."

It's not a coincidence that I chose this quiet café. Café Fénelon is the place where I fell in love when I was the same age as Ernest. Since my affair with that cold Swedish fish was not a great success, I decided that this time I'd choose a slightly warmer model. When I saw a dark and mysterious young man in the big amphitheater of the Sorbonne, I knew he would be the one. This law student, a mix of an exotic desert prince and Al Pacino. I couldn't identify his accent, but his irresistible smile charmed me immediately.

Gabriel turned out to be Israeli. I was 22 and very enthusiastic about studying at the prestigious Sorbonne. At the risk of sounding overly patriotic, I have to tell you that I'm very grateful to my country. I'm grateful to have studied in one of the best law schools in France. My professors were either ministers of justice, or authors of the law books French law students still use. I'm grateful to France because after finishing my studies, and my bar exam, I did not have to repay some giant bank loan. I didn't have to borrow any money. Not because my parents were rich (because they weren't rich at all); it's thanks to the French education system. I only paid $400 a year to have access to an excellent university. And that $400 even included my student healthcare.

Gabriel and I felt privileged to be students in the historic Latin Quarter. We were free and happy in Paris. And poor. Our first date was in Café Fénelon. Then, we used to study together in what we called "our café." I helped him with French law vocabulary, and he helped with my Hebrew. His level in French law was much higher than my level in Hebrew.

Of course, all my girlfriends were jealous of my good-looking boyfriend. But Gabriel was not only adorable; he was also very brave. He told me how he arrived alone in Paris when he was 18 without knowing a word of French. That was hard to believe since he told me in perfect French about an old black and white Hungarian film he had just seen. Paris was the world's cinema capital. In the Latin Quarter, you could see a silent movie from Murnau, the expressionist German director from the 1930s, or a Brazilian movie festival—all day long for peanuts. Gabriel's favorite director was Steven Spielberg. He was also working toward his PhD in cinema—at the same time he was studying law.

One morning, we were chatting over lunch in Café Fénelon. We didn't eat Portuguese oysters like Hemingway. Non. We were enjoying a delightful café au lait and a warm croissant. When you are in love everything seems delightful. My boyfriend was also brilliant. He succeeded at the Paris bar exam in one go—with excellent marks. But our story ended after university, probably because I had too much of a temper for a brilliant lawyer. I never went back to Café Fénelon until the day I wanted to have a conversation about Mister Hemingway's education.

• • •

"Bonsoir, Madame. Welcome! How are you tonight?"

There's nothing better than being recognized by the waiters at a chic café. Le Café Select is just such a café, so I'm very proud to be recognized when I have my coffee there. It's the first bar in Montparnasse opened all night since 1923. It was a must for the Bohemian crowd of this formerly artistic district. I'm giving a private French lesson and waiting for my student to arrive. I know what you are thinking: I'm now a French teacher? What about a tour-guide giving guided tours about Hemingway?

Well, it's a long story.

My ex-husband is half Canadian and half French, so he had a Canadian passport. He wanted to raise our kids in the country where he was also born and raised because "there's more nature in Canada than in Paris." I couldn't agree more. So, we were thinking of moving to Toronto where we both have family. It's funny, because Hemingway used to be a journalist for the Toronto Star, and he left his beloved Paris for Toronto, too. I thought I could be a French teacher in Canada because French is compulsory in school, as you probably already know.

So, at 40 years old, I went back to university in Dijon, Burgundy, and studied linguistics to get my license as a French teacher. But we never moved to Toronto, which was a good thing after all because I'm sure that, like Hemingway, I would have been very depressed so far from my Paris. And anyway, I couldn't imagine myself walking in the snow in my high-heeled shoes.

I'm at Café Select waiting for David. I always give my French lessons at Le Select because if I have to work, it might as well be in lovely places. And indeed, it's a wonderful place. Nothing has changed since the Roaring Twenties: the same mosaic floor, the same wooden chairs and banquette, the same stucco and molding on the walls, the same square tables, and the same chic, friendly waiters. There's even the same Art Deco toilets, and the same Welsh Rarebit that you can wash down with the same colorful cocktails mixed at the vintage bar.

Le Select is a Parisian institution. In the 1920s it was the hangout for American expats escaping Prohibition in the States. So, you can imagine how this place became the stomping grounds for these thirsty Americans.

The café is located just behind what was the new home of Ernest and Hadley in 1925, when they came back from Toronto with their baby, Bumby, and lived above a sawmill. Each morning, here in the café, Hemingway could enjoy his bread and butter without sawdust. And it's also here where the irresistible writer could kiss his lover, Paula, who would become Mrs. Hemingway Number 2.

The good times of the Roaring Twenties—sex, fun, and jazz. Hemingway wrote about this mythical café in his novel, "The Sun Also Rises." Brett Ashley is the cynical English femme fatale. She's constantly surrounded by Americans and horny men. Lady Ashley drinks in Le Select like a man, smokes in Le Select like a man, and chooses her many lovers in Le Select like a man. Nowadays, you can sip "The Sun Also Rises" cocktail here, and feel like you're also a decadent Hemingway character.

David, my student, is a nice Australian man in his sixties who retired in Paris. He's friendly and as he says he has that dry English humor. The only problem is that I don't always understand his jokes because I don't always understand his Australian accent. David loves Paris: the food, the mood, the cafés, the architecture—and the French women.

"They're so chic, so slim, and so sophisticated," he tells me with sparkling eyes.

"If you say so," I reply.

He confesses that he's looking for a Parisian girlfriend. Suddenly he asks me, "Teach me how to date a French woman!"

"Do you think I know?" I say. "If I knew how to date a French woman, believe me, I would write a book and become rich!"

But David insists. "You're a woman, you're French. You must know how I can date a French woman."

A few weeks later David arrived for his lesson much less enthusiastic about French women. "Who do they think they are? Miss Universe? So snobby and arrogant!" He complained they never smile. They always make faces. They act as if they were beauty queens even when they're plain. "In fact," he said, "I was wrong about French women. The English women I find here are much friendlier, and have a great sense of humor. French women have no humor at all."

David seems to forget that I'm a French woman. But I don't want to fight with my student, so I need to be diplomatic. And yet, I feel really offended that he's insulted my French sisters.

Finally, I smile. When you turn against the woman you used to worship, it's usually because you just don't understand her.

After the third French class, he tells me, "By the way, if you're looking for a lover, I'm here!"

I'm flattered but I don't know how to react. Maybe this not-so-subtle comment is the way men try to seduce women in the Southern Hemisphere? But I'm here to work, not to flirt with my student, even if he is mature, funny, and charming.

When David understood that his French lesson would never turn into more than French lessons, he ended his studies with me.

• • •

Then there was Christopher at le Select. Or Chris, as my friend Elizabeth, used to call him. Elizabeth is an American expat friend and modern art expert. She asked me if I could go around the city at night with her friend, Chris.

"He just bought a huge apartment near the Invalides," Elizabeth told me, her excitement coming through the phone. "He even has a real Miró painting. It's incredible! He's a plastic surgeon in L.A—and a great cook. You should see the magnificent parties he organizes here—it's sooooo incredible!"

Before you ask, no, I have never seen the apartment, as Elizabeth never invited me to the fabulous parties in the Parisian penthouse of Mister Incredible.

"But I'm supposed to attend a lecture at Shakespeare & Company Bookshop at seven-thirty tonight," I say. "There are more exciting things to do in Paris than hearing an American writer talking about his book, don't you think? He'll be bored with me, no?"

"Not at all!" Elizabeth says. "Shakespeare and Company is perfect. It's legendary! Chris will be thrilled to go to the mecca of the Lost Generation with you! He's single, by the way," she adds with a wink in her voice.

Since I'm newly divorced, I'm wondering if Elizabeth is up to something, choosing me to be Doctor Chris's Paris guide. I arrange to have him pick me up at six o'clock at Le Select. "After my French lesson."

I recognize him. He looks like his videos, the ones he uses to promote his clinic (yes, I confess, I searched for him on the internet to see what he looked like). He's about my age, tall and slim. Doctor Chris wears sneakers and casual clothes. I wave to him, and when he sees me, he smiles. I can see his perfect tanned face from the L.A. sun, and his perfect white teeth.

I stand up to faire la bise—kiss him on the cheeks like we do. He's a bit surprised that I kiss him on both cheeks. Well, we're in France, aren't we? I was not going to shake his hand. After all, he's Elizabeth's friend, and she's a refined modern art historian.

We chat. He orders a Martini, I order a Perrier. In fact, I'm the one who does all the talking because he's asking me so many questions about my life. If I'm married (not anymore); if I have kids (2 boys, 12 and 17 years old); what I do in life (tour-guide and private French teacher—when I can find normal students); if I was born in Paris (yes, in Belleville). The minute I answer a question, he immediately asks another. I'm wondering if he's going to ask me about my weight. (He doesn't.) Then he guesses that we are the same age, 53.

"If you were living in Los Angeles, you would have already started to do at least Botox injections twice a year," he says. "This is what I do the most in my clinic. I'm really successful with it. But you really look young. Congrats!"

"That's flattering, coming from you," I say. "It's like certain letters in Scrabble, your compliment counts double. The U.S. is a young country, so you like young women. France is an old country, so we like mature cheese, old wine, and mature women without Botox like me!" I say with a little smile.

Since I'm a polite person, I ask him questions about his life, too. He tells me he lives in Malibu (not the worst place to live). He loves hiking (that's why he's so slender and tan). He has a kind of girlfriend in L.A. It's not over, he explains to me, but it's not so great anymore. I'm glad to know about your love life, I think, but don't expect me to tell you about mine; it's not your business.

He's very confident. He speaks loudly with a warm, enthusiastic voice, and always smiles. Very friendly. I'm sure there is a waiting list in L.A. to be his girlfriend. He explains that he loves Paris so much that he decided to buy an apartment here so he can come here at least twice a year (like Botox).

"Elizabeth told me you own a Miró," I say. "How did you manage that?"

"My grandfather is from Philadelphia and he used to be Alexander Calder's best friend. You know, the artist with the mobiles. Calder came to Paris in the 1920s and he offered a Miró to my grandfather. There's even a private American Calder Foundation in France, which recognizes an artist in his honor every year."

"I didn't know that," I say "Your grandfather is like Hemingway! He also bought a Miró. I guess he liked the Surrealists."

"You know I have a strong sex drive."

"What?" That's quite a change of subject. I'm so astounded that I almost spill my Perrier. Why is he telling me this? I've known him all of twenty minutes, and he's giving me a resumé of his sexual habits? I don't care, and non, I don't want to know about his fabulous sex life. I have to check to see if anybody heard him, since I'm well known here. I don't talk about my intimate life even with my close girlfriends; it's my jardin secret. So why should I listen to the erotic fantasies of this guy I barely know?

I'm uncomfortable, but I don't want to be rude with the friendly doctor. Am I supposed to say, "Oh my God, you're the man I was looking for all my life"? Or maybe: "Your place or mine"?

Instead, I say: "So you're the opposite of Jack Barnes."

His expression says he was not expecting this answer. "Who's Jack Barnes?"

"The hero of 'The Sun Also Rises,'" I say. "Hemingway's novel. Jack Barnes, a war veteran, is impotent, which tortures him because he's madly in love with Lady Brett Ashley. He's the archetype of the Lost Generation, a disenchanted man traumatized by the horrors of World War I. Hemingway wrote a very famous scene between Lady Brett and Jake Barnes that takes place here, in Le Select."

Silence.

"Aright," I say dryly. "Let's go, or we'll miss the lecture."

• • •

I'm sitting on a very old wooden bench in the iconic Shakespeare & Co. Bookshop where Hemingway used to borrow books from Sylvia Beach. Well, okay, it's not the same exact place. They used the same name, but it's still just as iconic, from the 1960s.

The shop is very crowded. Chris and I had to queue with dozens of tourists. But I'm not really listening to the talented American writer explaining how he fell in love with Paris. A huge, literary spider just bit my thigh under my tights. While I'm scratching my leg furiously, I can't help thinking about the weird behavior of Doctor Chris. Who does he think I am? His future French lover to satisfy his demanding sex life? He's like Victor Hugo, who at 80 years old, was saying, "It's so tiring to make love three times a day."

Ah, I got it. Chris was thinking our meeting at Le Select was a blind date. Of course! That's why he wanted to know all about my intimate life. That's why I didn't understand his behavior. And why I was shocked. We were both victims of a cultural misunderstanding. For me, seeing Chris just meant having a coffee without ulterior motives with a friend of a friend who was lonely in Paris, nothing else. In Paris, love is in the air, so we don't need blind dates. The man of your life can appear anywhere. He can be the stylish man on the bakery line. Or the cute guy sitting in your favorite café. Or the intellectual reading a book beside you in the Métro. Or the seductive dog owner who's out at midnight when it's snowing, like you with your French bulldog. The man of your life can also be in the market on Sunday. He could be the charming man you see every week at the vegetable stand, the one who explains how he cooks the endives he just bought. Or the guy sitting next to you in a restaurant. And I didn't even mention the man at the party, the guest at a friend's dinner, the man at an art exhibition, or at a book signing or at Shakespeare & Co.

There is no magic nor surprise on a blind date. I can't imagine myself having a blind date even with a charming, tanned, rich, athletic American surgeon. Since I don't want Chris to have illusions about a future together, I change my behavior. After the lecture I stop laughing at his jokes; I quote French writers he doesn't know. In a word: I become a snob—distant, cold, pedantic, arrogant, and serious. Exactly how David, my Australian student, sees the Parisian woman. And you know what? I never saw Doctor Chris again, or his incredible Miró painting.

• • •

It's done. I've read "A Movable Feast" in English. I'm proud and very motivated. I decided to walk in the favorite garden of Hemingway: Le Jardin du Luxembourg. Hemingway used to come here with his baby. He used to talk about hunting pigeons in this garden with a slingshot then hiding the dead bird in Bumby's carriage. Le Jardin du Luxembourg is an elegant and quiet Parisian garden with lovely statues of all the queens of France. It's beautiful Medici fountain reminds one of Italy, and no wonder. The refined Italian-style palace in the garden used to be the home of the Florentine Marie de Medici. It's now the home of the French Senate.

It's weird. I can't imagine Hemingway hunting pigeons here. This chic place is not exactly Michigan's wild woods, where you hunt foul to feed your family.

It starts to rain. I search for a café to protect myself. I just have to follow Hemingway's path. I remember he wrote how, when he had an empty belly, he'd go to 12 Rue de l'Odéon, just next to the garden, where the iconic Shakespeare & Co. Bookshop was back then, but is no more.

Like Hemingway, I pass Rue de Vaugirard. This is the longest street in Paris. Under my umbrella, I see a plaque on a hotel wall and learn that Paul Verlaine lived here for a few months. I always look up in Paris. If you look up, you'll find hidden treasures, and learn about history. Verlaine is the cursed poet, poor but so talented. He probably died in the same building where Hemingway used to write, too. I'm sure the French poet sent inspiration to the young American writer.

I can see now, the Luxembourg museum where Ernest used to admire Cézanne's paintings. I even remember exactly where he mentions it; in the chapter called "Hunger is a Good Discipline." Hemingway explains how hungry he was and how that hunger changed his perception of Cézanne's paintings. I'm cold and hungry just like Hemingway was, and in the same place, too, but fortunately I'm not as poor. I'm not an artist, after all. I look up again, and this time, I see another plaque on the wall at 8 Rue de

Vaugirard. "Knut Hamsun. 1920 Winner of the Nobel Prize for Literature, worked here from 1893 to 1895." I'm wondering, "Who is this writer with a name like an IKEA chair?" If he won this prestigious Swedish award, he must be well known. A Swedish writer maybe? Hemingway won the Nobel for literature, too, but much later.

"I walk down the narrow Rue Ferou," Hemingway wrote. So, I go there. I pause a few minutes where Ernest lived with his lover, Paula, Mrs. Hemingway Number 2. It's much more comfortable and nicer than the apartment with a pot for a toilet, or the place above the sawmill he had with Hadley. This cozy apartment belonged to Paula's rich uncle. Paula Pfeiffer was a chic, trendy fashion journalist for Vogue Paris. I'm moved thinking that Hemingway saw, like me, the two elegant stone female sphinxes in the building's entryway. And I sigh. It's always the same story: a writer (or artist, or politician) becomes famous, suddenly he dumps the old wife and child and takes a younger, slimmer, richer and more sophis-ticated woman. Hemingway also swapped the devoted and dowdy Hadley with the fresher flapper, Paula Pfeiffer. The worst part, she was Hadley's best friend. They had an affair and got married in May 1927, in Paris. Never trust your best girlfriend.

At last, I arrive at the café.

Le Café de la Mairie is the only café in Place Saint-Sulpice. It's very well located. You might think this café is just an ordinary café. Maybe you wouldn't like it. You might think the furniture was probably bought in the '50s and is uncomfortable. You might not like the lack of space. For sure, you might be annoyed being so close to the next table that you can hear their conversation. You might think the waiters hardly smile. I won't even mention the toilets. No doubt, you would criticize the tiny bathroom. And when the time comes to pay, you might think your bill is as bitter as the coffee, and conclude that Café de la Mairie is overrated.

It's true there are no golden mirrors, elegant waiters, and stylish toilets perfumed with jasmine here. But Café de la Mairie is not an ordi-nary café.

When I come here, I always order a café crème. I immediately feel smarter when I drink this beverage. It reminds me of the literary ghosts who drank their café au lait here before me. I can see Henry Miller at the back of the café taking notes while smoking. I smell the tuberose perfume of Djuna Barnes, the elegant lesbian writer from the Roaring Twenties. I see her beside me, writing her up-and-coming book, Nightwood. If I'm lucky, I can hear the metallic voice of Jean-Paul Sartre. He's debating with the brilliant, handsome Albert Camus about the role of the intellectual in French society. On the terrace, I glimpse the shadow of George Perec, the French writer who had the amusing idea in 1969 to write 300 pages without using the most used letter in the French language, the letter "e." And when I'm in a good mood, I imagine I'm the heroine of the literary French movie that took place here, one that all Parisian customers know, La Discrète.

Indeed, Café de la Mairie is a soulful place.

As I sit here, I wonder how I can share all the interesting things I know about Hemingway in Paris. While I'm thinking, I'm trying to warm my hands on my steaming cup. I'll do a lecture here, in the luminous room on the first floor. It would mean everything to do a lecture in Café de la Mairie. It's less prestigious (and less comfortable) than Café de Flore, of course, but it's a humble and authentic café. It's the café of the poor intellectuals. Like me. The only problem is that my name is Madame Nobody. So, the café owner probably won't agree to it. Or he'll ask me for money to reserve the seats, and I can't afford that. That's if there are any seats to reserve. Because how can I be sure people will attend my lecture? What if nobody comes? Do I cry?

It took me some time, but I finally got up the courage to ask Monsieur Léon, the café's director, "if maybe, would he mind if…I was thinking of… would he agree to…" I tried not to be shy, and I asked him about my idea of doing a lecture in his famous café. He opened his big, black agenda, and asked, "When?"

I asked if I had to pay something, and Monsieur Léon frowned, shook his head energetically. "Of course not, madame! Why would you have to pay me if you bring me clients? We like to organize literary events in our café."

Fast forward a month later: Twenty people are staring at me. There are mostly Americans, friends, and friends of friends. I'm stressed when I speak in English about their idol, Hemingway.

"Cogito ergo sum" (I think, therefore I am) Descartes said. The meaning of this famous Latin quote is using doubt as a method to reject prejudices, to think by yourself and not take everything for granted. So, I followed Descartes's methodology. I had Descartes in mind when I went to Rue Descartes, the street where Hemingway used to write. Hemingway was from alcoholism, and misery. All through "A Movable Feast" Hemingway repeats that he was very poor while in Paris. No money to get a room under a roof, belly empty, no money to buy books at Shakespeare & Co, no money to buy clothes, starving in front of the nice Parisian bakeries.

But I felt there was something wrong. There were too many contradictions in his book. So, I started doubting Hemingway's life in Roaring Twenties Paris. If you're poor in Paris, you don't eat like Hemingway ate: oysters in cafés with Pouilly wine, or calf's liver (very expensive!) And how can you have a chef at home who cooks for you if you have no money? This is what Hemingway told Sylvia Beach at Shakespeare's. When you don't have money, you're not able to have lunch at Brasserie Lipp or Chez Michaud as Hemingway used to do. You don't go skiing in the Austrian Alps, either, and you don't buy a Miró painting. Non. And, ah oui—there is also his story of hunting pigeons in Jardin du Luxembourg. It's too funny. In such a sophisticated garden, hunting pigeons? And it's also quite amusing reading how Hemingway had to beg in the streets for milk for baby Bumby. Seriously, do you really believe all this? When you're looking for money to feed your kid, you work, don't you? You don't quit your job as a journalist in 1924 to write. And when you can't support your family, you don't go to Spain just to watch bull fights.

Then, there was the Norwegian, Knut Hamsun. I discovered him by looking up with my eyes in the street. Do you remember? He's a Norwegian writer who won the 1920 Nobel Prize in Literature. I found out that Hamsun had a huge influence on many Anglo-Saxon writers: the German Thomas Mann, the Austrian Stefan Zweig, the Swiss Herman Hesse, and the Americans Henry Miller and Hemingway. They all worshiped Knut Hamsun for his sense of psychology. Miller liked him so much that he wrote the preface of one of Hamsun's books, "Mysteries." If Hamsun is not very famous today, it's because he was involved with the Nazis. The most famous novel of Hamsun is "The Hunger." Hamsun writes how he used to be very hungry in Oslo, and how this hunger changed his perception of things because when you are hungry, you have different sensations. Does it remind you of something? Hemingway wrote, much later, the exact same thing in "Hunger is a Good Discipline," in the third chapter in "A Movable Feast." Now do you get it?

This legend of Hemingway starving in Paris is a joke. His being poor in Paris is not true. It's well known that Hadley and Hemingway had a very comfortable existence. Each month she had the equivalent of twice a Sorbonne University teacher's salary. Not so bad. Hemingway was well off in 1920s Paris, exactly like the majority of the other Americans.

I know what you are thinking. I forgot the high exchange rate of the U.S. dollar. Americans were rich in Paris when they were poor in the U.S.A. thanks to the U.S. dollar. This is what Americans and Canadians who used to live in the Roaring Twenties in Paris wrote in their memoirs. So, blame the dollar, not them. Those people were creative Bohemians in the City of Light, not rich idlers. But there is a little problem with their theory. It's not exactly the truth because they were rich idlers and not starving artists. How do I know this? Thanks to serendipity, I found a book in my little library called "Le mythe des écrivains à Paris, Ernest Hemingway et Henry Miller" (The myth of the American writers in Paris, Ernest Hemingway and Henry Miller). Too bad this book is not translated into English. The author, Daniel Gallagher is an American English teacher from a Parisian university. Mr. Gallagher has written something that does not lie. I don't mention what you read on the Internet or in memoirs. I mean the newspapers. Gallagher has read all American and French newspapers from the 1920s, and he created an interesting economic work. Gallagher talks about an economic phenomenon that curiously nobody talks about in this era: inflation. It's true that the US dollar was incredibly high, but France was ruined after World War I, and basic products were incredibly expensive, even if you were lucky enough to have US dollars in your wallet. Some essential French basic products increased in price 500%! Even the rich Americans in Paris were complaining. Ezra Pound said that he had to cook at home because Parisian restaurants were very expensive, and very mediocre. So, living well in Paris in the Roaring Twenties had a cost, and only rich Americans could afford it.

Why did Americans in Paris all pretend they were poor when they were not? Because of a song by Charles Aznavour.

I assume you know Charles Aznavour. He is a very popular French singer. He started as a poor Armenian refugee in France. Then he met his Pygmalion, Edith Piaf, and he ended up singing at Carnegie Hall in New York and had a national funeral in Paris. "La Bohème" is one of his most famous songs. It tells of the nostalgia of an old man for the Paris of his youth when he used to be a broke painter in Montmartre and was living the bohemian life. Aznavour sings the joy of being a poor young man but a talented artist. Young and poor but talented. Like the young Picasso who was starving in Montmartre but who created Cubism; like Modigliani and like Paul Verlaine, the miserable poet whose poems are taught at school. Hemingway reproduced the archetype of the cursed artist in Paris, Gallagher wrote in his book. Poor in Paris but a genius, like Aznavour's song. I'm a poor writer but I lived in the Jerusalem of the artists. I was hungry and I was cold in Paris but I made all these sacrifices in the name of literature for you, the reader.

In reality, most Americans in Paris were rich bourgeois but were creating the illusion of being poor, talented artists. How do you say cliché in English? The myth of the cursed artist in Paris sells well in the U.S. Guess which of Woody Allen's movies was the most rentable of his career? Yes.

"Midnight in Paris." I saw this popular movie twice. Allen made millions from this film. By the way, where are the French in the movie? The only French character is a French flapper, the actress Marion Cotillard, and of course the American hero played by Owen Wilson is in love with the Parisienne. The only non-American artists in "Midnight in Paris" are Dalí and Picasso, who are not very French at all. It's "Midnight in Paris" without the Parisians. In "The Sun Also Rises," too, the only French character is a prostitute. She has no dialogue.

Paris was the cradle of Modern Art in the 1920s. That's why Gertrude Stein came to Paris. So why is it that the Lost Generation never mention Parisian writers and artists in their books? Patrice Higonnet, a French history teacher in Harvard is also asking the same question in his book, "Paris: Capital of the World." Where is André Breton, the father of Surrealism? Georges Braque, inventor of Cubism? Kiki de Montparnasse, the muse of painters? The Jewish Russian painters from the School of Paris? The Dada Movement and Tristan Tzara? Cocteau? Matisse and Fauvism? They don't exist because Americans in Paris did not care about the French. They only cared for Americans.

In the 1920s Paris had five Anglophones publishers, printing English books, and English reviews. The most important review was "Transition," which had 4,000 subscribers. Americans in Paris used to live in a closed circuit and were reading their own books. Mr. Higonnet quotes T.S Elliot who advises American writers to use Paris as a home base, but not waste time with Parisians who deserve only superficial chit-chat in a café because they are shallow. The French historian concludes the only link between Paris and the Lost Generation was money. Eating cheap, drinking cheap in a lovely locale. This is why Scott and Zelda Fitzgerald came to Paris. Paris used to be Disneyland for American writers.

But there were other Americans who really liked Paris and the Parisians. They were speaking French fluently, they married Parisians, they opened shops in Paris, and they stayed in Paris when their compatriots returned home after the 1929 stock market crash. There were the African

Americans. They decided to stay in a country that treated them as human beings. Like the American Eugene Bullard, the first black American military pilot, who fought for France in World War I and World War II but was humiliated in his own country. Bullard became the owner of Le Duc, a famous jazz club in the Pigalle. Parisians loved the American musicians: Duke Ellington at the Moulin Rouge, Sidney Bechet, and later Armstrong. In Paris, nobody was paying attention to a black man kissing his white girlfriend in the street. But this same scene in the U.S would have been a cause for a bloody riot, and in some states, arrest. Yes, in the 1920s Paris was "le paradis" compared to America for black Americans.

The most famous of these artists is Joséphine Baker, of course. She became a French patriot and helped the French Red Cross feed the starving Parisians in the 1930s. In World War II, she joined the French resistance and later received a war medal from General de Gaulle. It's not a surprise that Joséphine Baker is still very popular among the French. What a (French) woman!

For me Hemingway is different from the other American writers in Paris. His love for Paris and Parisians was real, and he's not guilty of lying. Being hungry for Hemingway had different meanings. He was hungry for all the new things he could not experience in his American and puritanical world where dancing, smoking, drinking, and free love was forbidden. Hemingway was starving for life's pleasures, and Paris gave him that gift. It's in Paris that Hemingway was born, born as a writer.

When you read "A Movable Feast," you understand this book is a novel and not Hemingway's memoir. Hemingway wrote at the very end of his book, "it's fiction" and "don't be a detective." The writer never said "A Movable Feast" was his biography. It's the others who were mixing fiction with reality, novel with memoir. Even now some people make that mistake. Many of Hemingway's biographers are still writing that Hemingway was hunting pigeons in Le Jardin du Luxembourg or had to beg for money in the streets of Paris to buy milk for his son. The starving artist in Paris is still a highly marketable product.

Jules Renard, a French writer with a lot of esprit said, "Add three letters to Paris and you will have paradise." I agree, Paris is paradise. And take off the letter 't' from native and you'll have the word naive. Some Americans are naive when they have Paris in mind and some native Parisians are not.

Hemingway was always in movement. But one day he had trouble walking. His memory became weak. He couldn't write anymore. He became old. And a miracle happened. The Ritz sent him his chest, and like Proust with his madeleine cake, all his past came back suddenly. All his happy and carefree youth in Paris became alive. This elixir of youth gave him energy to write again. To write with the same style he used to write with when he started as a young man. The same dry, pithy sentences he wrote in 1926, he wrote again thirty years later. After thirty years he discovered himself. But when he was in his early sixties he was too sick to move. He had a major nervous breakdown and decided to leave. But Hemingway had not said his last word about Paris.

• • •

It happened on November 13, 2015. It's still fresh in mind, the horror of the terror attacks—130 dead, more than 400 people injured. And a few months before, the Charlie Hebdo and kosher supermarket attacks. We were all traumatized. We all had a relative, a friend or a friend of a friend who was killed. A few days after the attacks of November 13th, I had my morning coffee in my café around the corner from my home.

"You look pale," I said to my favorite waitress. "Are you okay?"

Sofia, who is usually smiling and joking with me, is mute. Her complexion is gray and she has big, dark circles under her sad eyes. She did not sleep well, I can tell; she probably was dumped by her boyfriend. I'm not worried for her, she is cute, she'll find another one very quickly. "My sister and her husband were waiters at Le Carillon. They've been killed. They had a six-month-old baby."

Oh. I feel so stupid. And I feel heavy-hearted. I'm so shocked that I really don't know how to answer.

"I'm so sorry! Oh it's so awful! What are you going to do?"

"We were thinking of going back to Romania, our country. But no. France is our home now. We're going to stay and adopt our niece."

Among the targets was the Bataclan, a concert hall, and several popular Paris cafés. The terrorists killed Parisians who were sitting on the terraces as a way of attacking the soul of Paris. For many nights, like other Parisians, I had insomnia, I was stressed out and depressed. My heart would race every time I heard a police siren. When I would say "au revoir" to my kids when they left for school in the morning, I would think it could be the last time, maybe I'd be killed in the Métro. Every time I thought about all those poor people killed, I would have tears in my eyes.

But I did not have the right to complain. I'd think of the families of the victims. How to react? How to resist? The motto of Paris is "Fluctuat nec mergitur" which means "it is tossed by the wave but does not sink" like a boat on the River Seine. There were terror attacks in Paris in the 1980s, too. But you can do whatever you want to Paris, even barbarians were not able to kill Paris, because Paris will always resist, will always stay alive. After the attacks in 2015, the way Parisians resisted was by continuing to go about their lives as they always did, "la vie parisienne." So, we went back to the café terraces. We were not scared. Well, me, I was scared, but I didn't let anyone see it.

The motto of the Parisian resistance was "je suis en terrasse" (I'm on the terrace). Many pictures of Parisians on café terraces flourished on smartphone screens.

On the TV screen there was also Madame Danielle Mérian. Again and again, this elderly woman was on every TV station, and on the internet. Even The New York Times wrote an article about her. When she was a child, Danielle Mérian saw photos of concentration camps that her father took. Since then, she decided to be an activist for human rights. This Parisian feminist became a lawyer who, even now, is involved in all the human causes from over the world. She was interviewed by BFM TV, a French news channel, where she put a rose in front of the Bataclan the day after the terrorist attack.

"It's very important to bring flowers to the dead," she said to the journalists in her strong voice. "It's very important to reread Hemingway's "A Movable Feast." We're a very old civilization, and we will uphold our values at the highest level."

Everyone was moved by this charismatic woman, and followed her advice. The French started to read "Paris est une fête"—Paris is a party—the French title of "A Movable Feast." In one week, "Paris est une fête" was sold out at all the Parisian bookshops, and on French Amazon. Hemingway's book suddenly became a bestseller in France. With his magical prose and his unique tone, Hemingway gave hope to heartbroken Parisians. Hemingway gave back to Paris what Paris gave to him when he was a young and unknown writer.

Six months after the attacks, there were huge posters everywhere, made by the city to encourage Parisians to go back to cafés and restaurants. It depicted three young women sitting in a Paris café and smiling, happy. And what slogan did they choose as their call to arms? "Paris est une fête."

It was everywhere: in Métro stations, on buses, on the sides of buildings—a book's title, full of optimism. Yes, Paris is a party. When I saw this poster, I knew Hemingway was telling me, "Don't be afraid. I'm here. Don't give up! The good old days will come back." Hemingway found inspiration in Paris, and Paris found consolation in Hemingway. And for that reason, I'll always be grateful to Ernest Hemingway. From the bottom of my Parisian heart, I want to say, "Merci Monsieur Hemingway!"

Chapter 4:

In Search of Marie-Antoinette's Teapot

"SO, DO YOU UNDERSTAND? YOU DON'T TALK ABOUT SEX, YOU don't wear heavy perfume, and you don't make jokes about nationality. And please, try not to get lost for once. It's a Very Important Client, a VIC!" says Michelle sternly.

Michelle is my boss; she owns a travel's agency in Paris. France is the number one tourist destination in the world, as you may know. Normally, Michelle is a warm woman with a strong personality and sense of humor, but right now she is not in the mood to laugh.

"Yes, don't worry. I'm a licensed guide. A professional," I answer, trying not to show her she's scaring me.

"I know, I know. But sometimes I'm a bit worried about you because you're a free spirit, clients love you but...well...anyway you are the only one who was able to do this visit. So, I will repeat again what I told you."

Yes, I remember: A famous American brand bought a French alcohol brand (sorry I can't tell you the name, confidentiality clause); the marketing team from America landed in Paris to learn about this French iconic beverage. They want to know how this product is linked to the French art of living. And my role is explaining the French art of living through the masterpieces of the Louvre. Great...Mona Lisa, Venus de Milo, and the Winged Victory are the well-known masterpieces of the Louvre. They come from Italy or from Greece, but not really from France. Michelle ordered me not to get lost in the Louvre. Easy! The Louvre is the biggest museum in the world—in the world! Eight miles of corridors, 403 rooms, 10,000 stairs, 430 windows, 3000 locks and 36,000 artistic works displayed; how can you not get lost in the Louvre? Yeah sure, this is going to be a brilliant visit. Ugh.

"Oh—I forgot to tell you. The CEO's secretary insisted that you have to talk also about Marie-Antoinette because one of his staff members is a big fan of the queen. And be careful because the big boss will attend your tour. Her assistant insisted, she said he is very demanding—friendly but demanding. Do you think you are able to do this tour?"

"Yes, no problem," I say. "Easy, don't worry. I have to rush now! Au revoir, Michelle."

No problem...easy...don't worry I'm telling myself in the elevator, leaving the agency. Everybody knows Marie-Antoinette never lived in the Louvre, but in Versailles. Everyone except the important CEO of this American company, apparently. But I can't be rude with the American big boss. I said that I was able to do this tour, but I lied. I'm not ready, and I start to panic. What I'm going to do? I'm super stressed.

I rush to the Louvre to prepare my visit and find inspiration among the French masterpieces. But of course, the room of French paintings is closed. Closed? Why? There is a strike, and nobody told me? How am I supposed to prepare my guided visit if the room of French paintings is closed?

When I ask a Louvre Museum guard, he answers: "Blame our president Madame! There is not enough staff in the Louvre so they cut the budget – that's why the room of French paintings is closed, there's nobody to watch it."

Then we start a conversation about the percentage of funds dedicated to museums in the French budget. It's a very interesting conversation, but I doubt that the CEO will be excited to learn about French public finances. The friendly guard advises me to come back on the weekend. "It's very crowded on the weekend for sure, but at least you're sure the room of French Paintings will be open."

Great! I'll have to give my tour for the Very Important Clients surrounded by hundreds of people and noisy tourists. Do you know how many people come to visit the Louvre? More than ten million every year. And I have a problem when I speak: I have a little voice. I don't know how to speak loudly. Sometimes on the phone people ask to talk to my parents thinking I'm a teenager. Shame on me. So, now the group won't even be able to hear me in the crowded Louvre. It's a catastrophe.

Non…I decide it won't be a disaster. It will be a triumph—my triumph. If my boss chose me for this delicate mission, there is a reason. I'm the best. She said it: I'm the only one at her agency who can explain history and tell stories. I was born a storyteller. I just need to be more self-confident. The VICs and the CEO will be so impressed by my guided visit that soon I'll have other prestigious clients. This is the tour guide's dream and the challenge of my life, and I'm going to succeed.

I went many times to the Louvre to prepare my guided tour. I learned by heart the French paintings. And I found Marie-Antoinette's heritage in Le Louvre. I have read many books about the origin of the French art of living. I'm super ready. The American kings of marketing are going to be dazzled by my artistic knowledge.

• • •

Café Marly is so well hidden that maybe you'll miss it. You'll have to visit the Louvre to find it. It's an enchanted place where huge, fluted columns lining flamboyant arcades protect you. You will feel powerful because you are in the French king's home. The Louvre, before being a museum, was the center of power for centuries, until King Louis the XIVth who decided to leave Paris for Versailles in the 17th century. Inside the café, the elegant, velvet decor harkens back to the time of Napoléon III. While you savor your coffee, you just have to look up to be seduced by the delicate, magnificent stone ceiling from Louis XIV's days. I don't even mention the view you'll have, which is breathtaking. All of the Louvre is at your feet. If you are cold, go inside the café. You'll be surrounded by elegant, red, flamboyant furniture.

I tried to be elegant today, too, because it is D-Day. I'm wearing a black pencil skirt paired with a black blouse, and shiny red sandals (with medium heels, of course, so I can walk miles in the museum). I'm walking in the direction of the glamorous Café Marly where the Very Important Clients are waiting for me. I'm terribly nervous; I have to be excellent.

I recognize them thanks to the efficient secretary who sent a picture of the big boss. Two men are sitting on steel chairs. In front of them, a refined woman is on a beige couch next to the big boss. They are all eating their desserts, except the big boss who is speaking on his ultra-modern-design phone.

"Hello, my name is Edith." I greet them with a big smile. "Nice to meet you! I'm your tour guide," I say with a friendly voice.

The two men smile at me, with mouths full of macarons. The big boss stares at me while he's speaking in English on his phone. The woman checks me out from head to toe. She is very blonde, very made up. She stands up to shake my hand. She is wearing a black skirt which shows her long, tanned legs. Her tight, striped, black shirt enhances her big breasts and her slim waist. And she has high-heeled black leather shoes. She is perfect. She reminds me of a Barbie doll.

She tells me, while she's moving her hands with her perfect polished white nails: "We haven't finished our lunch yet, and mister Gustavson is on a very important phone call right now. Come back in fifteen minutes."

"Fifty minutes?" I say, flabbergasted.

"No, fifteen," she says. "One and five. Excuse me but do you speak English?"

I apologize. "I didn't hear well. Alright then, I'll come back in fifteen minutes."

Alright? No, it's not alright. Does she not know how to say hello, sorry, and please? And she dared to ask me if I speak English, this rude woman? Could she not invite me to sit with them, and offer me a coffee instead of ordering me to leave?

I feel humiliated. Who does she think she is to give me orders? And who does she think I am? Her servant? I'm sure I have more degrees than this nasty woman.

I walk off, fuming mad. I need to calm down and behave like the professional tour guide I am. I can't show my emotions, otherwise I'll be unable to do my visit. But I'm very emotive. That's my problem in life. I blush for nothing, I have tears in my eyes for nothing, and I'm passionate for nothing.

Fifteen minutes are enough to find my magic potion. I run to the perfume store next to the Louvre and find it straight away. Pshhht! Pshhht! I'm now surrounded by a vanilla cloud. My favorite perfume cheers me up immediately. Ahhh, much better. Alright, it's time to work now. While I'm hustling down the street to rejoin my clients, I sing the song I heard in the perfume boutique: "We are the Champions" by Queen. Yes indeed: I'm the champion.

• • •

"Here we are, in the salon of 18th century French paintings," I say. "You'll be able to admire all the masterpieces that celebrate the famous French 'art of living.'" I point my finger at a painting. I try to be as enthusiastic as I can, have a strong voice, and be confident.

"The painter is Van Loo, and as you can read, and the name of this painting is "The Hunting Break." We can see men wearing lovely velvet blue jackets with bows and elegant women with satin dresses with bows, too. These hunters are having a chic picnic. A white linen napkin is laid on the grass, and we can almost smell the delicious patés." While I'm talking, the two men in the group are sending text messages, the assistant is staring at the ceiling, and the CEO is checking his phone every five minutes.

I wink. "And what are these aristocrats doing while they are eating and drinking wine in the countryside? They're talking. They are not focused on their smartphones. Eating and drinking well, while having the pleasure of the conversation. This is the French art of living. Conversation is an art in France, we call it 'l'art de la conversation;' the art of conversa—"

Ding Dong! Ding Dong! The Big Ben tower of London is ringing. Mr. CEO waves to excuse himself, takes a step ahead and starts to speak on his phone, turning his back to me. What am I supposed to do? I can't show him I'm annoyed by his behavior. He's not supposed to talk on the phone in the biggest museum in the world. He's supposed to listen to me, the French expert. But he's the client so what can I do? Nothing, so I pretend not to notice, and continue with my explanations.

"The 18th century is called the Enlightenment century. We say 'Enlightenment Century' because it's the century of science and philosophy. A new world appears, and people start to desire more personal freedom. Writers, philosophers, and scientists decided to light the darkness of the past, to light this new era. But—"

The CEO has ended his phone call and returns to the group.

"And that's why we call Paris the City of Lights! Because of the Enlightenment," interrupts the assistant. She seems very proud to show me, and the group, that she knows French history.

"Not at all, Madame." Touché! "Lyon is the city of lights, not Paris. We call Paris "The City of Light," without the letter S. It's light not lightsss. La Ville Lumière in French. It comes from the 17th century and not from the 18th century. Gabriel Nicolas de la Reynie, Lieutenant General of the police, was nominated by Colbert and Louis the XIVth to clean up the city, and obliged Parisians to put up lights. That's where the word light comes from. Alright now… let's see another painting…"

The little group follows me. The assistant is making a face; she did not appreciate my correcting her in front of her boss. She likes Mr. CEO a lot, I can tell by the way she's watching him all the time (when she does not sigh and look at the ceiling while I'm speaking). While they are looking at the painting, I'm watching Mr. CEO discreetly. He annoyed me with his phone call, but I must admit he's good looking. He has dark eyes and dark eyebrows. He must be in his late 50s, salt-and-pepper hair, not very tall but slender. And his voice is deep and warm when he talks on the phone. This is the first thing I noticed at Café Marly: his voice. He's wearing sportswear: navy blue chino trousers, a white shirt with a blue navy Barbour coat. He must be sporty; I can tell because of the style of his clothes and his legs. I like men's legs. Alright stop dreaming! Work now!

"You're selling a French beverage that was invented in the 19th century, but there is another French beverage famous in the world invented two centuries before and linked to the art of living." I stop in front of a painting showing elegant men drinking Champagne. This painting is "The Oyster's Lunch" by Jean-François de Troyes. But my clients hardly pay attention. How to get them to? "I guess you know who the most famous seducer in the 18th century was?"

"Giacomo Casanova!" answers Mr. CEO with a big smile.

What a smile. Perfect, white teeth and his hazelnut eyes sparkles when he smiles, exactly like Casanova. I'm not surprised the good looking assistant, whose name is Barbara, fell in love with Mr.CEO.

"Bravo, sir," I say. "And do you know in which language Casanova wrote his memoirs?" Silence. They don't really seem interested in Casanova now. I go on trying to entertain them.

"Casanova said the best part of his life was in Paris. He also said that making love has no interest if there is not an interesting and stimulating conversation before. The erotic power of the words. For the master of seduction, the art of conversation belongs to the art of love. And Casanova wrote his memoirs in French, not in Italian, because the European elite was speaking French, but also because he liked the French language." I motion to the painting. "I have another question for all of you: Why are there only men and no women in this painting?"

"Because men are coming back from the hunt," answers the young man of the group.

"Absolutely. But there is another reason. As you probably know oysters are an aphrodisiac. Champagne and oysters. With women it would have turned into an orgy." I take a step back. I have to wake them up. "But do you know how Casanova liked to eat his oysters?" I smile as they lean in. Now I have their attention. "By accident, Casanova let his oysters fall into the neckline of his charming female guest. He tried to eat the oysters, well, I'll let you guess how…."

I turn my head back to the group grinning even wider. But my smile fades instantly because I see that they don't seem to appreciate the way Casanova used to eat oysters. Catastrophe! The puritanical Americans are clearly making a face. I have to find something else to talk about, something without erotic allusions. I know! Marie-Antoinette. The assistant must be the one who loves Marie-Antoinette. All American women love Marie-Antoinette.

"Well…uh….we are going to see now a very interesting painting linked to Marie-Antoinette. Follow me please and be careful. We are going down to the first floor, so take care of the stairs. There is not a lot of space and it's an old stairway."

The four people walk slowly in the tiny corridor behind me. I'm not at ease, so I try to breathe to calm down.

"What is that smell?" calls out Barbara, the assistant.

What smell? I smell nothing except—damn! My perfume! I should not have doused myself in the store. She's right I smell like vanilla. A lot.

"I don't smell anything," I lie. I take a sniff and pretend to notice suddenly. "Ah, yes…you're right. I have no idea where it comes from. Maybe it's the Louvre? Perhaps they decided to put deodorant in the museum? Who knows? Maybe they thought a nice smell helps you appreciate the art?"

"Excuse me?" She does not seem convinced by my theory. Barbara comes up next to me as we are leaving the tiny corridor. "Oh…it's you who smells so strong. Mr. Gustavson is allergic to perfume. I told your agency. Why didn't they tell you?" She frowns with her thin and perfect eyebrows.

Oh, how stupid of me! I forgot I wasn't supposed to wear perfume. I watch Mr. CEO reading his text messages. Again, on his phone. He must be sleeping with his phone, and with Barbara. He seems perfectly fine and not bothered by my perfume. Fortunately, we've arrived at our destination.

"We are in the room dedicated to the painter Elisabeth Vigée-Lebrun," I say. "She is one of the rare female French painters." I'm in front of one of my favorite paintings. A self-portrait of Vigée-Lebrun embracing her little daughter, Julie. I can feel the tenderness and the love between mother and child. It's so moving. But I have to talk about Marie-Antoinette, or Barbara will be disappointed.

"Vigée-Lebrun became the favorite painter of Marie-Antoinette because she invented Photoshop, meaning she knew how to make people more beautiful. For example, for Marie-Antoinette, Vigée Lebrun had the skill to recreate the delicate, pale complexion of the French queen." The group is examining the delicate and lively portraits. They seem to like it as much as I do. Hopefully they forgot Casanova and his erotic oysters.

"Didn't she paint the portrait of Marie-Antoinette's lover?" Mr. CEO asks.

"Sorry, but who are you talking about?" I ask.

"Fersen, the handsome Swede!" adds the assistant glancing at her boss.

I'm impressed by Barbara's knowledge. Not only is she gorgeous but I have to admit that she knows Marie-Antoinette's life very well. Not many people know who Fersen is, a sexy Swede and the only love of the French queen. "Well, we don't know if they were lovers, in fact. Elisabeth Vigée-Lebrun did not paint Axel de Fersen," I say. "Alright, follow me please. Now we are going to end with the sophisticated interior design from the same era."

While we're walking in the direction of a corridor, Mr. CEO comes alongside me with a little smile, and whispers in my ear with his deep and sexy voice: "You are wrong young lady! You are wrong about Marie-Antoinette and Fersen! They did have an intimate love affair."

Alright, at last the big boss dares to talk to me but it's only to tell me I'm wrong! I am wrong? Since when is this American CEO a French historian?

My first reaction is to take a step away from him. My perfume! If he smells my heavy perfume, he'll have an allergy attack, and he'll sue me for sure. Americans sue people for nothing. I sigh. He gets on my nerves. He thinks I don't know who Fersen is? Of course, I know. Close companion, but I don't believe they were lovers meaning they had an intimate relationship in a bed. Marie-Antoinette was never alone; she was the queen of the most powerful country of Europe. How could have they slept together? Fersen and Marie-Antoinette were enamored with each other, sure, and we have their love letters, but sex between them? I personally don't think so, based on my own research. Fersen had other affairs, he was very seductive. But he worshiped only one woman: the queen of France. For Fersen, his love of Marie-Antoinette was not the same as her love for him. Fersen venerated Marie-Antoinette because she was the queen of the most powerful kingdom of Europe. Marie-Antoinette loved Fersten like a teenager.

"I don't agree with you, sir," I tell Mr. CEO, with a self-confident, but respectful tone. I'm keeping my distance so he can't smell my vanilla fragrance.

He comes up next to me, leaving the others behind. I can feel he wants to talk with me. With a little smile I add, trying to be funny, "If you knew Swedish men like I do, you would be sure nothing physical happened between the last queen of France and the Swede."

"You intrigue me," he says. "What do you mean 'know Swedish men like you?'"

Alright, he is not my good friend, so I'm not going to tell him about my disaster with Björn the Swedish nuclear physicist. But I can't help telling him Fersen was a cold man. Even if Fersen had affairs with many other women, there was no love, no passion, no emotions with his lovers. And thoughtlessly I answer: "You know…I used to have a Swedish boyfriend, and like Fersen, he was warm…like ice. I used to call him IKEA's 'fridge.'"

As soon as I finished my sentence, I realized I'm ridiculous. I'm supposed to be a professional art historian who talks about paintings, not a pathetic woman revealing her intimate life to a client in a museum. This is the story of my life. I'm too spontaneous, I never think before speaking, as if I have no filter. And I'm unable to keep my distance with people I like. And I do like him. He is very charming, very mysterious. He does not behave like most American men I meet. He doesn't shout when he speaks; he is not too sure of himself, and he doesn't smile too much.

Now he has an ironic glazed look, and his eyes sparkle.

"Young lady—"

Why does he always call me that? It gets on my nerves; it's condescending.

"—I know all about IKEA," he says, "because I, like the 'cold Fersen' and your cold Swedish boyfriend, am also an 'icy' Swede."

I blush; I hear my heart pounding. My vision blurs. He's Swedish and nobody told me? I'm an idiot. I did it again! I made a stupid joke about nationality, and I upset him. My boss talked to me about American clients, not Swedish ones. I thought Mister Gustavson was American. Obviously, I got it wrong as usual.

I have to say something nice to him. But I'm embarrassed and humiliated. How do I respond? How do I cover up this faux pas, me, the queen of goofs?

"Ah? You are Swedish? Really? How nice…eh…I like Sweden very much." I stammer, hopeless. "Well…now…let's end with Marie-Antoinette's teapot. Follow me, please."

The two young men and the assistant are moving in my direction.

Alright, let's go to the 18th century interior design section. It's on the left...no it's on the right. I look at my watch. I have ten minutes more. Wonderful, and we're not even close.

Akhenaton and Nefertiti Room

This is what I see written on the wall after five minutes of walking.

"Can you tell me why we are in the Egyptian section?" asks Barbara with a dry voice.

She is sexy—and smart. She noticed I was lost. Yes, why are we here? She is right, we are not supposed to be in Egypt. I'm feeling like Dora the Explorer but I don't have Boots the monkey to help me, or a map. I'm lost in Egypt.

"Well...as you are selling alcohol, I thought you would like to learn that Egyptians invented beer."

"Where are the toilets?" asks the younger man.

What? The toilets? Do you think I know where the toilets are? Do you think I had two hundred hours of art history at university to know where the toilets are in the Egyptian section of le Louvre? No. Now, I'm feeling like Moses with the ten plagues of Egypt. What will be the next plague? Fortunately, I see a guard. I ask him in French, discreetly, for the location of the toilets. And suddenly, like Moses, a miracle happens, the red sea opens in the Egyptian section and I see in big letters: 18th Century Decorative Arts Gallery

I sneak through the crowd, and like a shepherd dog, I bring my little herd in front of a big showcase. The chic travel suitcase of Marie-Antoinette is in front of us. Everything she needed when she was traveling is here.

There is a wicker vanity case lined with red satin. Inside there are plenty of delicate objects. Her objects. The group admire all the beautiful products of a fashion queen: the small powder box, the moisturizing cream pot, tiny crystal perfume bottles, a pestle to grind her blush. The same products a modern woman still needs for her morning beauty routine. And here is the teapot! A small, white porcelain teapot engraved with her pink monogram: MA. And the porcelain cup and fragile saucer, and the tiny tea filter with silver spoon and adorable sugar box. It's so delicate, it looks like a tea set made for a doll. But it was made for a queen, the last queen of France. All the sophisticated, dreamy world of Marie-Antoinette is around us. We all are moved, even me, who is used to seeing her royal universe.

"Oh my God! Oh my God!"

Every two minutes, Barbara shouts, "Oh my God!" Why does she have to shout to express her emotions? She is spoiling the mood with her exciting and acute voice. Does everybody have to share her overwhelming enthusiasm about Marie-Antoinette's objects? She really gets on my nerves. She makes me think of a schoolgirl in front of a candy shop. If she says, "Oh my God!" again, I'll push her down the Henri II stairs. And tomorrow in Le Parisien newspaper this headline will appear on the front page:

"American Tourist Dies in the Renaissance Stairwell in the Louvre. French Tour Guide in Custody."

Better than the Da Vinci Code.

Ding-Dong, Ding-Dong!

No! Again, the tacky Big Ben bell. Now it's Mr. CEO who is spoiling the mood with his phone. Before he can answer, a female guard rushes over shouting in English with a strong French accent.

"Monsieur! Yes, you! It is forbidden! Phones are strictly forbidden in the Louvre!" The woman looks so angry that I don't even have to translate for him.

Like a little boy, Mr. CEO shakes his head, and puts his phone in his pocket. "Oh, so sorry," he says sheepishly. I had to laugh. This important man is reduced to a child scolded by his mommy.

I continue the tour to take the attention away from Mr. CEO. "You are going to see now the royal watches, here, in gold, diamonds, malachite and topaz." We all move into a small adjacent room.

The guard is following us. While the group is admiring the watches that look like jewels, I walk over to the lady guard and I tell her in French, "Thank you for telling him to stop with his phone. I can't bear this kind of behavior. Because he has a lot of money, he thinks the Louvre is an annex of his office!" I'm aware that what I'm saying about the Swedish CEO is mean, but he humiliated me in my favorite museum with his stupid comment about IKEA's fridge. The Louvre guard avenged me.

"You're welcome," she says. "It's normal, it's my job. I agree with you, I can't bear it either."

"He didn't even listen to a word of my tour; he was always using his phone. And what a stupid ringer he has: Big Ben! His ringer alone shows he has no education. Money does not make up for class. Why do these kinds of tourists go to museums?"

"For selfies, I guess," she says, laughing. "Their big egos need a museum as big as the Louvre."

Mr. CEO is watching me while I speak with the woman. Maybe he realized that I exist? Maybe he has a crush on me? Now he's checking his watch since he can't use his phone anymore. Yes, indeed, it's time to leave. I tell the group the visit is over, and I show them where the toilets are. They all thank me.

Mr. CEO comes along beside me. "Thanks, Edith, it was a very interesting visit. Would you like to join us for a hot chocolate at Angelina? You deserve it," he adds with his irresistible smile and sexy voice.

He says all this in perfect French. And I realize that he's understood me all this time—including every snide comment I made about him to the guard. That's why he was watching me!

I turn cold. My heart starts beating wildly again. I need air suddenly. I can't feel my legs anymore.

I need to escape. I make some excuse to leave, wave goodbye to the others, and dash away without another word. I climb the Henri II stairs and fly out of the museum.

Mortified, I run to the closest café I can find.

On the other side of the street, Le Café Nemours is waiting just for me. I fall into an empty chair and order a coffee.

I'm shaking. Mr. CEO never gave away that he understood the awful things I'd said about him. Instead, he was smiling at me.

I feel stupid and ashamed. And soon I'll be poor because I'm going to lose my job. Not only did I do everything wrong during my visit, I insulted an important client.

What am I going to do? I can't call my boss; she won't understand. Barbara will be so happy to complain about me. I'm sure my boss, Michelle, is going to fire me. I'm waiting for her text message. I'm sure it's coming any minute. She's always very quick and efficient. I know exactly what she'll say:

Are you crazy or what? Did you lose your mind? Talking to them about sex? And why did you insult the boss? Her assistant complained about your behavior. She said you were arrogant, disrespectful and you did not even know where you were going. You wasted their time. I'm very sorry but I have no other choice but to end our working relationship. Michelle

I check my phone, nothing. I look up and see a plaque on the wall: Place Colette. This is the name of this beautiful square. Suddenly, I think about her, about Colette, the famous French writer who used to live, and who died, just next to this square. Colette is the first female writer who had a national funeral in France. What a woman. She made a huge scandal showing her breasts and kissing a woman in 1907 on the Moulin Rouge stage. She was an artist, a journalist, and a popular writer. She had younger lovers, she had female lovers, and she did not give a damn what others thought of her. She was an audacious and free woman.

Then I see the tobacco shop in front of the square. The sign says, "A La Civette, Since 1716." It's where George Sand, another famous female French writer, used to buy her cigars. Her cigars! A woman who was smoking in public in 1830! George Sand used a man's name, used to wear men's trousers when it was strictly forbidden, and she was involved in politics, which was unheard of at the time for a woman. She was a scandalous woman, too, and could not care less. She was the iconic free woman of all Europe.

I think of these women, and I decide that I won't cry. Non.

Me too. I'm a free woman like Colette and George Sand. They are both my role models for life. I'm outspoken, I don't play it safe. "Je suis comme je suis," sings Juliette Greco, the muse of Sartre. I am what I am. I will find another travel agency that will appreciate me and new clients who will like my authentic style of tours in the Louvre. Voilà!

"Allo? Mon chéri?"

The tables of Café Nemours are so close that you have the feeling of sharing your coffee with your neighbor. If the woman next to me says "my darling," she must be talking on the phone to her lover.

"Have you done your homework? I'll be home late. I need to work at the office, darling. The food is in the refrigerator. Mummy loves you."

A single mother, this is what she is. Her "darling" is her son. And I realized that I'm exactly like her. I'm also a single mom, and I work hard. What will happen to my two sons if I can't work anymore? We won't have a home anymore; we will end up in the street. I'm not Colette, nor George Sand, I'm only a future unemployed tour guide with no savings in the bank.

Cling!

This is it, it must be my boss's text message.

I knew it. Now I'm going to cry....

Chapter 5:

A Romantic French Lesson

MONDAY.

I'm late. I hate being late. It's not polite; it means my time is more precious than yours. But it's not my fault. My son was sick during the night, nothing serious, but I hardly slept. I have big, dark circles under my eyes. I'm exhausted, I'm in a bad mood, and it's not the day to arrive late.

Here it is, Place des Vosges. I'm almost there, five minutes more. I'm always mesmerized by this beautiful square, one of the most elegant in Paris, and one of the oldest. Tall windows, red bricks, high and identical buildings – it's not surprising this district used to be the place of the rich and famous of the 17th century. They got rid of the vegetable gardens and the swamp, and they built, instead, their magnificent mansions. But the name of the swamp stayed. Le Marais—the marsh—is the name of this beautiful and well-preserved neighborhood.

But Place des Vosges is not the original name of this VIP place. Until 1800, it used to be called La Place Royale—Royal Square—to mark the engagement of the royal fiancés: Anne of Austria and the French king, Louis XIII. That was in 1612. Today, it is one of the oldest squares in Paris, yes, but hardly the most austere. In the time of Louis XIII, if you were looking for a lover, it was the place to be. So, Place des Vosges is the ancestor of online dating.

Right now, though, I'm not running after love, but after business.

At last, I've arrived: Carette. My favorite tea room in the Marais. Like Place des Vosges, where it's located, this tearoom is discreet and chic. It's late October, so it's too cold to sit outside. I told him "inside," and he is inside. I can see him in the reflection of the storefront window. He is really not bad...not bad at all. Relax. I take a big breath for confidence. Why shouldn't I be confident, after all? He has money, he has power, alright, but I'm in my own country. Paris is my city. The man who is waiting for me to get his first French class is not an ordinary client. My new student is Mr. CEO. That visit to the Louvre with him and his staff was a huge disaster. I don't even understand what I'm doing here now. I was supposed to be fired because of him, not be hired again thanks to him. That's why I'm so uncomfortable. I feel humiliated. I just want to forget him, forget that awful episode at the museum. But, come to think about it, things didn't happen how I expected. I never received a text message from my boss after my awful visit. Nothing. I went on my other guided tours as if nothing happened. And then, six months after that nightmare, I received an email from my agency:

The American CEO of the alcohol company is back. He is in Paris for three days and he wants a French teacher every day for a private French class. Since you are also a certified French teacher for foreigners, I thought about you for the job. If it's fine with you, I'll send you the details later.

What could I say?

Dear Michelle,

Thanks for your message, but it must be a mistake. I was ridiculous and pitiful during my Louvre visit. Please don't force me to see Mr. Gustavson again, I'm too ashamed.

No, of course. I could not say this to my boss. So, instead, I answered:

Ok! it's fine, thanks. I'm waiting for your instructions.

And here I am. Six months later.

I can see his back. Even his back is attractive. Calm down. He sat on the chair to let me have the banquette, which is the height of chivalry.

1 point.

He did not order yet because he's waiting for me.

1 point.

He stands up to shake my hand when I arrive.

1 point.

I can tell he's a gentleman. An attractive gentleman.

"Good morning, sir, how are you?" I say. "I'm so sorry to be so late! My son was sick during the night. Were you waiting a long time?"

"It's ok," he says. "Please sit. What do you want to drink?"

"Eh…a Darjeeling tea please." I'm shocked. He doesn't even ask me how my child is? Not even pretend he feels sorry for my son? How selfish he is!

Minus 2 points.

"So, I brought this book for your French class," I say. I place it on the pink marble table, "Alter Ego 3: Méthode de français." "I hope you'll like it," I say. "I always use it, and my students are very satisfied. You'll learn grammar and lots of French vocabulary."

"I'm sorry, Miss, but I think you didn't understand what I told your boss. I don't want to use a book. I don't want to learn grammar. I don't have time. I'm in Paris for just three days. I only want a French conversation class."

I want, I don't want…What a bossy man he is. I hate it when men give me orders, especially when it's my field—and French language is my field. But he proposed to pay twice my normal fee because I was immediately available. He's a businessman, so no time to waste. I can't complain. I'll make a huge effort to bear this spoiled student. Two hours a day for three days. Not bad after all. But how am I supposed to give him a French conversation class if I don't have a book or something written? I need to think fast and be smart. This student has zero patience, I can tell.

Tick tock, tick tock…I have an idea!

"Could you please introduce yourself? In French, I mean," I say.

"Oui…My name is Erik with a K, Erik Gustavson. I'm single. I'm 62 years old and I live in San Francisco."

He is 62? He looks much younger. He is Californian. I'm not surprised, that's why he is tanned. And he's fit, too. I'm sure he has a private sports room in his penthouse. He is like all the Californians who are crazy about their bodies. I'm sure he is vegetarian and gluten-free. Healthy and wealthy. I prefer New Yorkers, always in a hurry, stressed and grumpy—like me.

"I'm American, but I was born in Sweden. I've lived in San Francisco for more than thirty years now. I'm divorced."

So Barbara the assistant is not his wife, so, his partner maybe? Alright, not his partner either, she is the lover.

"I own different companies," he says. "One, a distillery, the other, a software company in Silicon Valley."

I already knew he is an important CEO, but I did not know about the other company. His French is good. He hardly makes mistakes; he has a light accent. It's the first time I've heard a Swedish accent in French, and it's charming.

"Could you please tell me, Erik with a K, what do you like in life?" I ask.

"I love the ocean, that's why I live in San Francisco. I was born in Stockholm, in Sweden—"

Thanks for telling me where Stockholm is located, do you think I'm stupid? I know a bit about European geography.

"Stockholm is near the sea," he says. "I used to work on a fishing boat when I was young. In fact, I'm still just a simple Swedish fisherman, at heart."

A simple fisherman, of course. Who wears a Lacoste Polo, a Cartier watch, and Ray Ban sunglasses. Alright, now what else can I ask him? I have to find something French and cultural for the simple fisherman's conversation. Tick tock, tick tock…yes, I know!

"Do you see this painting?" I say. I turn my back and point to the only painting in the tearoom. "What can you tell me about this painting? What do you see?"

"Let me see..." He surveys the painting. "It's...a woman, a woman from the past. She has a nice red dress, but she is not my type. She's not very sexy."

Ha, ha, ha. Not funny. Swedish humor, I guess.

"She is more than sexy, sir, she is chic," I say. "She's a chic woman from the 17th century. You can tell because of her clothes."

"Sorry, I don't know much about fashion. It's shallow girl's stuff."

This man is hilarious. According to his own point of view. But I'm a polite French teacher, so I force myself to smile...a little bit.

"And what do you see behind her in the painting? Do you recognize the scene, Erik?"

I try to be friendly. He seems to have adopted the American habit of calling people by their first name, but for me it's not polite and it's over-familiar. I hate it. But I have to make an effort, or he'll tell my boss I'm an arrogant French teacher.

"Yes, I recognize the square, Edith. It's where we are. Place des Vosges."

"Voilà! Exactly," I say.

I have to speak less quickly. When I'm enthusiastic I speak too fast, and I'm enthusiastic right now because I like the woman in this painting very much. I'm not like my student, who is placid. If I speak French too fast, he won't understand a word, and he'll complain to my boss. I have to tell him the story of the woman in the painting. Her name is Julie d'Angennes. She was born in Paris in the beginning of the 17th century. What is important is her mother, Catherine de Rambouillet. She created the first literary salon in Paris. It was located in her mansion at l'Hôtel de Rambouillet, just next to the Louvre. And it was in her bedroom where she used to receive the crème de la crème among writers. It was the blue bedroom: la chambre bleue. In the 17th century women from nobility used to receive guests in their bedrooms. It was normal. Even the queen used to receive important people in her bedroom. Catherine de Rambouillet taught French men to be gallant with women, not to be vulgar, and not to smell like garlic. Thanks to her French education, men started to recite romantic love poems to ladies. Catherine had a daughter, Julie, the woman of the painting. Around 1630, in the blue bedroom, Monsieur de Montausier fell madly in love with Julie. To seduce her, he invented a refined book with poems. Each poem was composed by the best writers of the time. Every page of the book was decorated with a different flower. It was Julie's garland—la guirlande de Julie. Even now, a gentleman still uses the language of flowers to express his feelings to a woman he loves. But Julie was a bit spoiled and her fiancé had to wait fourteen years to marry her. She was the one. For the love of your life, wouldn't you wait a bit? When they got married, they lived just here, exactly where I and Mister CEO are drinking our beverages. Isn't it extraordinary? Those sophisticated, educated women created with other refined Parisians a well-known literary movement. Because they knew their own value they called themselves Les Précieuses, The Precious Women. Madeleine de Scudéry is the famous writer among them. She invented the Map of Tender, la carte du tendre. A hit! It's a geographical map of feelings between a man and a woman. Sweet friendship, love, passion, tenderness, affection or...cold indifference. Love is an important concept in France. I guess that's why people call French the language of love.

"Very interesting! It's almost twelve. I'm hungry, let's have lunch now." He grabs the menu. "Order what you want. It'll be my treat."

He makes a sign to the waiter who dashes over.

This man knows what he wants. He is very sure of himself, and very efficient.

"Oh, thanks," I say. "I always take the vegetable pie here, une quiche aux légumes. You won't be disappointed, everything is fresh."

"Sure, I'll have the same. And what to drink? A glass of wine?"

"I don't like wine. I'll have mineral water please."

"A French woman who does not like wine? How can it be?" He scrutinizes me.

I feel like a little girl who made a mistake. What does he mean? This man intimidates me. I'm not at ease with him. I don't really know if he likes my conversation, or if he's just polite. I can see he is not really fascinated by my story of the blue bedroom and love in French literature. I guess he's more interested in the stock exchange than the refined Parisian women from the past. It's hard to know what he has in mind because he is serious.

After a few minutes, an elegant waitress with a perfect white apron brings us our quiches and drinks. The quiches are warm and smell divine. My serious student gives me the first plate. He then takes my glass and fills it with mineral water. He drinks his wine like a connoisseur. I'm wondering if this place is elegant enough for him. He must be used to eating in Parisian palaces. Maybe he's not happy to be here, but he doesn't say a word. Great! Mr. CEO has zero sense of conversation. There is a big silence. I feel less and less at ease. I have to find something to talk about. Let's see if I can master the art of conversation better than my mute pupil. "How is your quiche? And your wine? Do you like it?"

"Yes."

How am I supposed to conduct a conversation if he answers in monosyllables?

"I was wondering something—" I say, "—French language is not very useful in life. Plus, you don't really need French for your business. So why did you want to learn French? And where did you study French? Why do you speak so well?"

"A lot of questions to answer," he says. "Thanks for saying my French is good. I'm flattered." He looks very serious. "Why French in my businessman's life? Well…it's a long story. My mother always worshiped everything French: the country, the food, the language, the culture. I guess France used to be seen as very exotic in Sweden. Then she met my French father. He came from France to Sweden as a car designer for Volvo. But he dumped my mother when she was pregnant with me. He left Sweden before I was born and never acknowledged me. It was in the fifties, you know. She had to raise me on her own. She had a lot of grief, but no bitterness. She wanted me to know about the culture of my unknown father. I do know that he came from Marseille. I hired a private detective when I was 18 years old, and tried to contact him, but he wasn't interested. Turns out, he had another big French family."

Incredible. Mr. CEO becomes more talkative! Maybe he is becoming more comfortable with me, for him to tell me his life like this? I feel sad for him.

"Oh, I'm sorry," I say, "but you don't really need French language lessons. Your French is perfect!"

"Maybe my French is not bad, but I know nothing about France. I used to be a rebellious teenager, and I was more interested in Swedish girls than French culture. At 21 years old, moved to the U.S. to study business and economics. I stayed there, and I never found time to learn about your beautiful country."

He pauses, sighs. "You know…I spent all my life making money, and I can tell you, I was quite good at it. But now I want to feed my brain, not my wallet. And if I don't learn a new thing each day, I feel like my day is ruined. That's why I liked your Louvre visit. I wanted to thank you, actually. I learned a lot that day."

Ugh, the Louvre visit. Why does he have to remind me of that? He wants to thank me? Is this his not-funny Swedish humor again? He doesn't look like he's joking. Is he talking about another tour guide? It's like the Twilight Zone. Mr. CEO and I were in the same museum, but not on the same spatio-temporal "episode."

"Maybe my knowledge is not so bad about the paintings, but not for Egyptian culture. Egypt is not really my favorite subject," I tell Mr. CEO while putting my glass of mineral water to my lips. My subliminal message to him is: I know I was not great, but you know what? I don't care.

"Of course, I noticed you were lost in the Egyptian section," he says. "Don't look at me with this furious look, it was a good thing, you know. You really made me smile and I don't usually smile a lot in museums. It's a visit I will remember. I did many guided tours at the Louvre and in Paris before, plenty of times, believe me. My tour guides were always very knowledgeable, but I never had such a funny guide. You were so amusing trying to find your way in the museum. And thanks to you I learnt how Casanova used to eat oysters…I love oysters."

Funny? Me? A funny guide? Who does he think I am? Funny Girl? I'm not a "funny guide"! I am an intellectual Parisienne. For sure, I'm less sexy than his charming assistant. But I can't be rude with this rich client, so again the fake smile, pretending I'm flattered.

He probably knows that I didn't appreciate his comment because he adds immediately: "And you really made my day. I was very glad to meet Nefertiti again."

"You're welcome. Are you interested in Egypt?"

"Not really," he says. "I'm only interested in Nefertiti. I went to Berlin many times for business, and each time I take time to visit the Nefertiti bust at the Berlin Museum."

He takes his ultra-modern smartphone from his grey velvet jacket pocket. He shows me his mobile's background. "Look, this is Nefertiti."

I start laughing. "Too funny! You seem to really like her!"

"Like is not the right word. I'm fascinated by her," he admits. "I always visit the Berlin Museum for at least an hour, just to admire her perfect face. Have you seen her? I am so impressed by this gorgeous Egyptian queen that I have goosebumps each time I see her."

It's funny how Mr. CEO is so enthusiastic, suddenly. I can't believe the uptight businessman has goosebumps for an old Egyptian statue. Nobody is even sure it's a real one. Some art historians say the Nefertiti bust at Berlin is a fake. Maybe I should tell him? No. I don't want to ruin his fantasy.

"Once when I was at the Berlin Museum, I had vertigo and I had to sit because I was overwhelmed by Nefertiti. This had never happened to me before. So, I was extremely happy to meet her again here at the Louvre… thanks to you."

"Oh, I see. You experienced an aesthetic shock. You had 'Stendhal's Syndrome.'"

"Excuse me but which syndrome?" he asks, looking puzzled. "I didn't get that."

Stendhal is a very famous French writer from the 19th century. All the French teenagers know Stendhal because they have to study his most famous book "Le Rouge et le Noir" in high school. "The Red and the Black." He wrote a lot about love and relationships between men and women—again, a French author who wrote about love. Stendhal even wrote a book just to analyze love, and guess what its title is? "De l'amour"—"About Love." He was a soldier in Napoléon's army at just 17 years old. It was not his real name. It was his nom de plume. Henri Beyle was his real name; he took his pseudonym Stendhal from a German city where Napoléon's army stayed. He was thinking that a writer is a man who knows the human's heart. In the beginning of the 19th century, Stendhal was in Florence. He loved Italy. He went to visit a cathedral and saw Giotto's frescoes for the first time. He was so mesmerized by their beauty that he had vertigo and became sick, exactly like Mister CEO in front of Nefertiti in Berlin. Here is what Stendhal wrote:

"I was in a sort of ecstasy, from the idea of being in Florence, close to the great men whose tombs I had seen. Absorbed in the contemplation of sublime beauty. I reached the point where one encounters celestial sensations. Everything spoke so vividly to my soul. Ah, if I could only forget. I had palpitations of the heart, what in Berlin they call nerves. Life was drained from me. I walked with the fear of falling."

[From Stendhal's book, entitled "Naples and Florence: A Journey from Milan to Reggio."]

Everybody has known, at least once, the same experience as Stendhal in Italy—in Paris, or in Berlin, felt physically the beauty of a perfect landscape or an artistic masterpiece, and almost fainted.

"I'm glad to learn I caught the Stendhal syndrome. It's fascinating! Sorry, but I have to rush now!" He asks for the bill. He pays with cash. I'm a bit surprised by his dry behavior. With a nervous gesture, he takes a wallet from his grey velvet jacket's pocket, removes a handful of banknotes, and he gives me the money.

"This is for you. Really sorry but I must go! Here is my phone number." He gives me his business card. "Send me a text message to tell me where to meet tomorrow. Merci, au revoir, young lady. You did not disappoint me." He leaves.

This man is not a man, he is the wind. He does things so fast. He seems always in a hurry; I wonder if he sleeps at night. I try to decode his behavior. I repeat his last words: "You did not disappoint me." What does that mean? Did he like my class? Mystery. I guess he did…a little bit. Maybe…who knows? Otherwise, he would not have asked me for another lesson tomorrow. This man is weird—he's cold, and he hardly smiles. It's a pity because he has a charming smile. At least he liked Stendhal. But he seems less warm than other people who live in America. Probably because he is from Sweden. But he is generous, I tell myself, while I count the money he gave me. A huge tip! I had students who were more attractive, but this man has something more. He has charm and charisma. Alright, I have a lesson to prepare for tomorrow. Back to work! Enough dreaming about your charming pupil. What am I going to teach him tomorrow? And where? Oh! I know!

• • •

Tuesday.

Here I am, just on time. Odeon Métro. I climb the stairs from the station. I see him. He is just near a big statue.

"Bonjour, Madame le Professeur. How are you?"

What a cute accent in French. He seems to be in a good mood. He is wearing a navy blue jacket with the gold buttons. The same one he wore in the Louvre. Around his neck, an electric blue wool scarf.

I'm in a good mood, too. In one hour, it will be dark, but the sun is still shining now; it's late afternoon.

He really is attractive; a seductive, mature man. But I'm a dreamer who mistakes her wishes for reality. Stop dreaming! Remember? He has his Barbara, the beautiful and smart assistant you can't compete with. So, like a mantra, I whisper to myself in my mind: He is not for me, I'm not for him, and I master my feelings. He is not for me, I'm not for him, and I master my feelings. It's quite efficient. I have to talk to him only about French history and literature, and nothing bad will happen to my marshmallow heart.

"Do you know who this man is?" I point the statute next to us

"Of course." And reading the plaque, he says with a somber tone, "Georges Jacques Danton, Minister of Justice from 10th of August to October 1792. Well, this Monsieur Danton was a justice minister only for a very short time."

"Danton is one of the leaders of the French Revolution," I say. "He used to live exactly here, as did other Revolutionary leaders. You see, it's also written, one of his quotations: 'After bread, the first need of the people is education!' He was right. He ended badly, like many. He was guillotined. Before dying, he said to the executioner, 'Show my head to the people. It's well worth seeing.' This district is linked with the French Revolution. In front of us, in the courtyard, the doctor Guillotin tested his machine. Doctor Guillotin used to be the doctor of Louis XVI's brother. He tested the first guillotine with sheep. Equality for everybody, even in the face of death."

"Oh…scary," he replies, touching his neck. "So, are we in the 18th century today?"

"Absolutely. Today we will time travel to the 18th century. Look—" I show him the café in front of us. "Do you see the name of the café?"

"Le Café Danton."

"Now you know why it's called Café Danton. Shall we go?"

"To Café Danton? Already?"

I laugh. He can be funny.

"No! Walking! Today it's not a French class, it will be a guided visit—in French!"

"Good idea. Let's go."

We arrive in a square; in front of us there is the majestic theater with prominent, white Greek columns. "Here we are in La Place de l'Odéon, and this district is named for this theater, Le Théâtre de l'Odéon. Marie-Antoinette inaugurated this prestigious place in 1782. The 18th century is really the century of theater. It was extremely popular. Here, a popular playwright of the time debuted his work. It was in 1784."

"Five years before the beginning of the French Revolution?"

"Absolutely. And it's not a coincidence. There were many philosophers and writers who were against the privileges of nobility, who wanted freedom. Voltaire, Rousseau, Diderot, among the most famous that you probably know."

"Yes, I know. The Age of Enlightenment, you told us about it at the Louvre. You see, I was listening to you even though I was on my phone."

"I can see. Anyway, Voltaire, Rousseau and the others never saw what their philosophical ideas had provoked, because they all were dead in 1789 when the French Revolution started. It was the end of the Ancien Régime. It was the end of the monarchy and the beginning of our first Republic," I explain.

About this famous and popular play in 1784. Here is the plot: A man is the servant of a count. This servant is in love with Suzanne, who is the maid of the countess. The servant wants to marry Suzanne, but the count wants to sleep with Suzanne, too, in the name of a feudal right, the "first night" right. (He is a count, so he has this kind of privilege.) Of course, the servant is angry with him and does not accept it. He wants to marry his beloved Suzanne. Love, again. But the author of this play did not write only beautiful love stories, he also wrote about the freedom to love who you want. This was a revolutionary concept. This writer used theater as a platform to criticize the privileges of the monarchy

"So, let's see if you know your classical music. This play even inspired an Italian opera, although the composer was Austrian" I say, having explained the plot.

"Mozart?" he offers.

"Yes, Mozart! But the name of the opera?"

"'The Marriage of Figaro!' I saw it at La Scala in Milano a few years ago. "Le nozze di Figaro." The name of the hero, the servant, is Figaro. But it's by Mozart not a French writer."

"Beaumarchais wrote the 'Marriage of Figaro.'"

"Bo who?"

"Pierre Caron de Beaumarchais. An Italian, da Ponte, wrote the words for Mozart's opera. But he was inspired by the 'Marriage of Figaro', written by the French Beaumarchais. Have you ever heard of him?"

"No. Never been introduced to your Monsieur Bomarshie."

"Beaumarchais! Pierre Carron de Beaumarchais. This man was incredible. He is very well known here, the king of theater! Light, funny, but also critical of the abuses of royal power. Just his life is incredible. He had a very lively biography. He started as a humble watchmaker in Paris, then he became a secret agent for the French king in London. He was harp teacher for the daughters of Louis XV. In the end, he was a very successful writer for the stage. Beaumarchais also sent guns and ammunition to the 25,000 rebels in America. He helped them win the famous Saratoga battle."

"Very Interesting!" he says. "A French writer helped the Americans in the war against the British? That was very nice of him."

"The French like freedom the same as Americans—la Liberté. Talking about freedom, the Marriage of Figaro sent its author to jail. Beaumarchais was sent to the Bastille for a few days. And Danton, do you remember him?"

"The man of the statute, the beheaded minister of justice?"

"Yes, exactly. Did you see him on the platform when you came here? He has his bust on the subway platform of Métro Odeon."

"No, sorry. I never take the Métro in Paris."

I'm not surprised. Parisian Métro is probably not sophisticated enough for Mister CEO.

"Danton said Figaro killed the nobility," I say. "Now follow me, please." I lead the way onward.

We climb the stairs of the theater and enter a small marble gallery on the left. It's the artists' entrance. We are alone. It's getting dark, night has arrived, and the gallery is not well lit. Everything is so quiet, peaceful. We don't even hear traffic outside. The mood is very romantic. The old lamps give the illusion of candlelight. This old-fashioned gallery is magical. We are back in the 18th century. We are both speechless. I can hear my heart beating.

I'm not for him, he is not for me, and I master my feelings…

Be focused on Beaumarchais! He smiles at me, and what a smile. I like his beautiful teeth. "But you're freezing, young lady! Let's go now. You deserve a hot chocolate."

Good idea. As we leave the theater, I see a poster on the door. "Wait! Look. How funny. They are going to do a play by Marivaux next month here. 'Les Fausses Confidences'—'The False Secrets.'"

"I have no idea why that's funny, sorry. Anyway, let's keep going, it's cold."

We walk in the direction of Luxembourg Garden. It's where you'll find one of my favorite cafés in Paris: Le Café Rostand.

It's very windy. I should have brought a warmer coat. I close my tiny jacket under my coat and I raise my collar to protect my neck. But I'm still very cold. Suddenly, he takes his wool scarf from around his neck and gives it to me.

"Take it! I'm a Swedish sailor, I'm not cold."

"Oh…no. It's fine, thanks."

"I insist!" His voice is very deep, very assertive. Well, I guess I have to do like he says. He is my boss, after all.

I take the scarf. It's so soft. Cashmere. I glance at the label: Dior Hommes. He has taste. Interesting, it smells of…nothing. A French man would have a French perfume on his scarf. I would have not complained if he had put his elegant scarf around my naked neck. A French man would have done this. French men are romantics, they know how to behave toward a woman. Vikings are cold. I'm not for him, he is not for me, I master my feelings…

"Have you ever heard of Marivaux?" I ask. "The man on the poster?"

"Mareewhat?"

"Ma-ree-vo," I pronounce it carefully for him. "Pierre Carlet de Chamblain de Marivaux. He is another famous playwright. In fact, there are two from the 18th century: Beaumarchais and Marivaux. But Marivaux was born before Beaumarchais, and his work was performed in 1735, when Beaumarchais's work was performed in 1785, fifty years later." I tell him how much I like Marivaux. He's so modern. "Marivaux wrote only about the feelings between a man and a woman. About love…again…"

"And you really think writing about love is new and modern?" He is talking with a bitter tone, ironically, as if he's angry. "Love is a bad thing. You become weak and stupid when you're in love. I was in love once, many years ago, and it almost ruined my life, and destroyed my family. Never again. You French are naïve romantic dreamers. Talking and writing about love all the time."

I halt in my tracks. He does, too. My Marivaux? Not modern? I can't believe it. I must defend my favorite writer. It's a question of French honor. And why is he telling me about his love life now? This man is cynical. Plus, he doesn't get my Marivaux.

"Of course, Marivaux is very modern!" I say. "The way he writes about love is very contemporary. In all his plays, there is a man and a woman who are not in love at the beginning, but they fall in love by the end. At the beginning, both characters don't even realize they're in love.

And when they realize, well, it's too late. They fight against their feelings; they don't want to be in love, but Marivaux decodes the heart's language. It's he who invented the French expression meaning to fall in love, tomber amoureux, a play on the expression to fall ill, "tomber malade." Marivaux thought that just as you don't choose to be ill, you also don't choose to be in love. You fall in love. Marivaux understood that love is like a sickness because you can't control your feelings."

"Alright, that's interesting," he concedes, "but it's not 'modern' to me."

I won't give up. He needs convincing. "And he also gave his name to a French expression we still use today, 'le marivaudage.' This was even used while he was alive. At one time it had a negative meaning, because it meant to use pretentious language. It's exactly the same complaint that people had, a century before Marivaux, against Les Précieuses. They were also criticized for their refined language. Today, this expression isn't negative anymore. Marivaudage is a double entendre where you use words to seduce. In fact, Marivaux invented the art of seduction. Seduction is an art because it's very subtle, and not everyone masters it. And in 2016, this play, 'The False Secrets' became a movie with one of our most talented and modern French actresses, Isabelle Huppert. And you say that Marivaux is not modern?"

I realize I'm speaking loudly. "Sorry, I'm talking too much."

At last, we arrive at the café. I have to calm down, or he'll think I'm an overbearing French teacher. I'm so focused on pleading for the modern Marivaux that I almost forgot I was cold. I'm relieved when we arrived at the café and it stops the conversation. I'm too emotional; he probably thinks I'm crazy to let something so little get on my nerves.

Le Café Rostand is crowded. But I have been here so many times that this elegant café has no secrets, and I know where to find a place for us. "Let's go to the back."

Two hidden leather armchairs are waiting for us.

He calls the waiter over to order. As we are seated comfortably, he says, "I think your idea of the art of seduction is a Latin concept, not Anglo-Saxon. The Americans don't know the flirting game. The way men and women seduce each other is more direct; It's the same in Sweden. You don't waste time in the U.S. In Scandinavia, either. And it can even be dangerous. In the U.S., you can be sued if you are too aggressive with a woman."

"I'm sure you master the art of seduction very well," he continues. "Me, I'm very bad at it. It's Barbara who seduced me. She told me later that she was in competition with other women from my firm. She was not the most attractive among them, but she was the most audacious. I like American women because they're not scared to get the man they want. French women are definitely too complicated for me. Me, I'm an old, boring Swede."

He tells me in English that the French class is over, looks at his luxury watch. "Do you have to leave?"

"Now? No. I'm still much too cold," I say.

"I'm glad you're cold...so you can stay with me."

Our hot chocolates arrive. We wordlessly turn our spoons in the milky beverage.

What does he mean he's happy I stayed? I think. What is this change coming over him? He doesn't have to dash off like a thief in the night for some meeting this time?

"This is yours," I take off his blue scarf and I hand it to him.

"Merci, Madame." He smiles at me, a big smile this time.

How can I resist him?

He puts his scarf around his neck, putting it to his nose. "I can smell vanilla. It's your perfume. A lot of vanilla."

"Oh, sorry. I know you're allergic to perfume," I say. "Your assistant told me at the Louvre. She was angry with me. She even shouted at me."

"Barbara told you I was allergic to perfume? Oh, I see. Not really. I'm allergic to her perfume, a strong patchouli that gives me headaches. I asked her to change, but she says it's an aphrodisiac," he says. "I'm very sorry if she shouted at you. She can be a bit tough sometimes. By the way, what's the name of your delightful perfume?"

Why does he want to know? Now the serious capitalist businessman is interested in women's perfume?

"Habanita, by Molinard, 1921," I say. "It was used in women's ciga-rettes in the Roaring Twenties. And it was so popular that they made it into a perfume."

"The Roaring Twenties. I'm not surprised. It suits you; you're truly a woman from another era. I can tell that you like the 1920s. And which men's perfume do you like?"

"Oh many," I say. "But my favorite is Pour un Homme by Caron. It's very classic. Its creator chose the name, For a Man, because it's not for teenagers. It was made in…" I try to remember "in 1934, I think. I also like Santos by Cartier. Cartier, like the brand of your watch, am I right?"

"Yes, you are. Bravo. You told me that Beaumarchais used to be a watchmaker, right? I'm like your Pierre Caron de Beaumarchais, I do like watches. I have a big collection. It's my weakness."

"Oh, interesting! Beaumarchais was so smart. He invented a clock system that Swiss watch firms still use. Do you have any Swiss watches in your collection?"

"A few. Philippe Pateck is my favorite. I also like Blancpain, Baume et Mercier—all from Geneva. Uh-oh" he is checking his Cartier watch. "Already 7:30? Sorry," he says, predictably. "I have a Skype meeting with a real estate agent from Spain. I have to leave."

Voilà! I was sure he would leave quickly. Fortunately, I finished my hot chocolate. "Sure, no problem. Business first."

"It's not business. I want to buy a house. I told my real estate agent to call me when he finds something with a big swimming pool. I like swim-ming. I'm a Swedish sailor as I said. I like the water."

"So why don't you have a boat instead of a house in Spain?"

"I had a boat. I sold it. I bought a house in the forest in Sweden, instead. Where are you going? I go west."

"Uhm, I go south."

"Alright, I'll pay for your taxi," he offers.

A taxi, I'm not made of sugar! I'm a strong woman, I can take the Métro. I stand up to put on my coat. He stands up too, and rushes to help me. What a gentleman!

"Oh, merci! It's very nice of you, the taxi, but no." I shake my head. "I can take the Métro. I'm used to it."

"I insist. It's dark and freezing out."

We're in the street now. It's cold, cold, cold. I try to warm myself as best I can. He waves his hand and in one minute, a taxi stops.

"This is for the taxi, and this is for you." He gives me an envelope. I give him a big smile to thank him.

"You know who you remind me of when you smile?" he asks. "Claudette Colbert, the Hollywood star from the 1930s." He opens the taxi door and I get in.

Just before closing the door, he adds with a serious look, "Good night, Edith. It was a charming French literature class. See you tomorrow." And in a very deep voice, he whispers to me, "Vous êtes dangereuse!"

Chapter 6:

At Midnight on a Bridge

I LOOK AWFUL. I SLEPT BADLY, BUT NOT BECAUSE OF MY SON this time. I could not stop thinking in the taxi, at home, until midnight:

"Vous êtes dangereuse." "You are dangerous."

Why did he tell me this? Me? Dangerous?

Anyway, he can't be interested in me, dangerous or not. I'm nothing to him. He's rich, I'm poor. No, he is not just rich, he's very rich. I looked up the brand of his favorite Swiss watch, Philippe Pateck. Cheap watch indeed! I almost fainted when I saw the price: 100,000 euros! He does not have one very expensive watch, but a collection! Not to mention his house—houses plural.

So, why me? Why would he care? He can have a top model—any glamorous beauty from California that he wants. I'm sure the gorgeous sirens from Malibu would want him, like Ulysses, the Greek hero. So, why would he be interested in me? His life is already wonderful. He has the money, a life under the sun, houses, cars, watches. And Barbara, the gorgeous assistant.

Vous êtes dangereuse.

What did he mean by that? Maybe I'm dangerous because I'm a risk to his perfect world? Maybe Mr. CEO and the Clumsy Parisian Tour Guide act like two characters from a Marivaux play. In all Marivaux plays, the man and the woman think they can master their feelings, but in the end, they master nothing, and can't help falling in love. How will Act III of our play end?

"Only the language of love will talk," wrote Marivaux. The double meaning of Marivaux. It's exactly what happened with Mr. CEO. When he was with me on Monday and Tuesday, he spoke and acted one way. But I'm sure he was thinking another way. I could feel it.

He behaved as if he was rigid, cold, serious—and not attracted to me. This is what he wanted to show me. This is what he wanted me to think. But my intuition tells me that he has feelings for me, that he wants to hide his emotions. How do I know? Again, thanks to Marivaux: the language of his heart. Erik couldn't help it, but a few times yesterday, his heart spoke to me. He said that I'm a smart woman, and that he likes smart women. In the café, he was happy I was cold so I could stay with him a little longer. He also said I'm very French—that the way I speak is very French, and I'm charming. I know he likes everything French because my boss told me so about six months ago, during our briefing. Then there is Claudette Colbert, the cute and playful French actress from Hollywood that I remind him of. Of course, I know her. I love all those old black and white Hollywood movies. She won the Oscar for best actress for her work in the great, romantic Frank Capra film, "It Happened One Night," with sexy Clark Gable. I adore Capra films.

His last words…his last words…before leaving me last night: Vous êtes dangereuse. It was as if it was a confession of the heart. His brain said "no" but his heart said "yes."

But what about the language of my own heart? I can hear what it's telling me: I like him a lot. For more than two days, I was constantly thinking about him. It's a sign. When I returned home from my first class, the Métro was very full, yet despite this hell, I was in heaven. Another sign. My heart beat quickly; I had butterflies in my stomach when I saw him yesterday. Another sign. There are so many things I like about him. He seems interested when I tell him about Paris history. Few people are interested in History and even fewer share my way of seeing life—life through Paris. I decided to live my life through the prism of Paris. Not the trendy Paris with the trendy and modern places. Non. I live in the Paris of the past.

It's my strategy to see "la vie en rose." I live my life through literature, art, and through the history of Paris. Each stone, each street, each monument, each museum, and each café can tell you a different story. I'm a vintage Parisian who smells of mothballs. This modern world does not really interest me. You know, the Internet, Twitter, Facebook, Instagram, TV, video games, Netflix, or even modern movies. I don't care. It's all just pictures, speed, and screens. There are no books, no paintings, no classical music anymore. We live in the image era. Have you seen the people in the Métro? Most of them are addicted to their screens. Those of us who still read books or newspapers in the Métro are the minority. People don't have time anymore. They're always busy, but busy doing what? They do things instead of thinking about things. Every time I want to see a friend, she must check her electronic agenda to plan one month in advance—just to have coffee with me.

But this man is different. He likes it when I talk to him about history and French literature. He is a listener and I'm a talker. He is a real gentleman, too. It's so rare! He is also smart. I like smart men. He is seductive. The alpha male. Virile, a deep voice, self-confident but sensitive and sweet and humble—and funny in his own way. I can feel he's as sensitive as I am. I noticed the way he watches me sometimes, as if he was trying to restrain himself. His heart is away from the light. He's protecting his heart from suffering, so much that it could be difficult for him to confess his feelings for me. That's why I'm a dangerous woman. I'm putting his heart in danger. That's why he fears me.

But I'm scared, too. If I use my conscience, my reason, and my brain—of course, I'm scared. We are not just different; we are exactly the opposite. It won't fit; it's a waste of time. I'm spontaneous; he's passive. I'm on the moon; he's down to earth. I'm an artist; he's a businessman. Normally, I like artists or intellectual men: writers, painters, comedians, musicians, or teachers. I have nothing to do with the money-makers, even though I respect them.

But maybe we are yin and yang? Different yet complementary? No, I must be lucid. How can I compete with Barbara? Of course, she's not stupid. She is actually pretty smart. At the Louvre, she knew more French history than I thought. How could I be the rival of Miss America? But if…

Alright, enough dreaming. I'll see him at 8 o'clock because he was busy with meetings all day with his Singapore office. I've never been to Singapore before and I will probably never go to this exotic island.

What am I going to wear? For two days with him, I wore the classic outfits of a classic French teacher: black skirt and a white shirt. I was anxious to meet Mr. CEO. But today, I'm not nervous anymore. I decided to be me. But I shouldn't do too much, or he'll notice I made quite the effort, and of course he'll think I did it all to please him.

No, I have to be subtler. It's the last day I'll see him so it's now or never. Black and white will be perfect again. I am giving a French class, not an Argentinian tango lesson. I have to be sober, but chic. Standing in front of my closet, I wonder which skirt to wear. Let's try this one. No, it makes me have a big bottom. This one? Even worse. It gives me a belly. This one? Too short. It looks like I have big calves. What about this one? Oh, too tight. I can't breathe. I really need to stop eating croissants for breakfast. What's the time? Oh no! It's 7:30pm. Now I'm late again. Alright, I'll take this skirt, but what about the top? Too late to change again. I'll keep on what I already have. It will be fine. Oh! But it's my pajama top! I stayed home all day in pajamas. But, if I put my leather skirt with it, nobody, even Mr. CEO, will guess it's a pajama top. I put on a long jacket to hide my croissant-addicted butt. Shoes? If I have high heels, I'll feel feminine and powerful. I have exactly 20 minutes now to get to the Métro. Rushing with high-heels booties. Makeup? No time. I'll do it in the Métro. I check my purse for my moisturizing cream, mascara, and purple lipstick. It will be fine. If I wear too much makeup, he'll think I want to seduce him. Or worse, that I'm an easy lay. Anyway, I'm old fashioned. If he doesn't make a move, I won't either. Time to run! Fortunately, it's direct from my home. Only 10 stops.

• • •

He is waiting for me at Saint-Germain-des-Prés, next to the church door. I'm supposed to teach him a philosophical text from Sartre. But no, I don't want to tell him about Left Bank intellectuals. I want to tell him about poetry because our world doesn't have enough poetry. I want to tell him about a love poem.

But first, I take him in the tiny square next to the church, to admire a statue.

"Why is it written to Guillaume Apollinaire when this statue is a woman's face? Guillaume is a man's name." he asks me.

I reply, "Because it's Dora Maar, Picasso's lover. Picasso's best friend was Guillaume Apollinaire. This sculpture is by Picasso. It's Dora's face but it's dedicated to the prince of poets, his friend Guillaume Apollinaire."

We stroll around Saint-Germain-des-Prés. I show him the artist studio of one of my favorite painters, the great Romantic painter from the 19th century. Picasso called him a "bastard" because he had to admit this leader of the Romantics was a genius: Eugène Delacroix.

Mr. CEO tells me I am like my monsieur Delacroix, a Romantic Parisian woman.

"I guess so," I reply with a smile.

It's time to eat. We choose Le Procope, one of the oldest and most elegant cafés in the world, in continuous business since 1686.

"I'm hesitating between a croque-monsieur and boeuf bourguignon," I say as we peruse the menus. I explain that the croque-monsieur has a double meaning. Of course, he knows that a croque-monsieur is two pieces of toasted bread with cheese and ham and a kind of Bechamel sauce. But he does not know the double meaning. Croquer means "to bite" in French. It's also a verb linked with love.

"When you like someone very much," I say, "you say you would like to bite on him. So, un croque-monsieur is more than toasted bread." Of course, I told him about le croque-monsieur on purpose. I never intended to order it; it was just an excuse to talk to him about love using the double meaning of the language.

He asks if there is the equivalent of a croque-monsieur for men.

"Oui! Of course. Le croque-madame," I say. "It's the same as a croque monsieur but with an egg on the top." The double language of Marivaux.

"Maybe I should have a croque-madame," he says.

"Maybe. Me, I'll have boeuf bourguignon. It's delicious and it's my favorite."

He orders the same, then tells me I am a food expert.

During the meal, since I am still technically his French teacher, we go on talking about French. But I talk about love again, of course, and explain that the French worship two things: love and food. "There are many love expressions linked with food," I say. "It's very interesting from a linguistics point of view. 'Having the heart of an artichoke,' for example, means to fall in love very quickly and very often."

We start laughing. Again, the double meaning of language.

He smiles when he sees how much bread I am eating during the meal, and smiles even more when I tell him I could live without love but not without a baguette.

We drink red wine from Burgundy. I have a glass just to please him because he does not want to drink alone. It is a very good Bourgogne. We talk about our lives. He tells me he had visited many countries around the world, he tells me about the fabulous cruises he did in Venice on a friend's boat, and on the Danube River, and in Norway. Of course, in Sweden, he used to sail with his own boat. He tells me about his favorite palaces around the world. I am fascinated. And impressed too. He also tells me he can advise me about his favorite five-star restaurants in Paris.

"Even a coffee in those prestigious places isn't affordable for a humble guide like me," I say.

At the end of the meal, we chat in English with the people sitting next to us, a nice couple from Shanghai on their honeymoon in Paris.

While we are speaking with the Chinese couple I'm thinking that Mister CEO does not know that I speak Chinese. Alright not very well to be honest, but enough to have a small talk. So I suddenly ask them in Chinese if they like Paris and what did they prefer to visit. The couple answers to me in Mandarin that they love Paris and the Orsay museum is their favorite place to visit. I tell them that I'm a tour guide and Orsay is also my favorite museum in Paris, all this in Chinese… of course. The couple looks surprised that I talk to them in Chinese but it's nothing compared to Mister CEO. Suddenly, he becomes speechless. When the Chinese couple leaves, he asks me, "You speak Chinese, too? Why? How?"

I shrug and tell him with a placid tone, "I like China very much, I visited it three times so I decided to learn how to speak, write, and read Chinese. But it was a long time ago, you know, and unfortunately, I forgot all I knew."

"Still…I'm very impressed. You are really a woman full of surprises."

This time, it was me who impressed him!

He suggests we get dessert at another café because he doesn't like the touristy café.

As we leave, it is raining hard and, of course, we don't have an umbrella.

"Stay here," he tells me. "I'll be right back."

I stay in the restaurant and after twenty minutes, he returns. I really feel sorry for him when I see him. The rain thoroughly soaked him.

"This for you," he says, handing me an umbrella. "Let's go now."

I think to myself, "No man has ever braved a storm to find me an umbrella. Ever. This man is not a man; he is my knight. I'm a lady from the Middle Ages and he is my courtly lover.

Because it is raining, we don't walk far. Under our umbrella, we duck inside the first café we saw—a chic place. It is a cozy place, but with this storm, any place would seem cozy.

"I love crème brûlée," he says, happy. "Let's see if they have my favorite dessert here."

They do and he is very pleased. "Would you like to share a glass of wine with me again? Please say 'yes.'"

"Again? Well, I don't really like drinking wine, except one: Champagne."

"So, let's drink Champagne." He orders a bottle from the waitress. "With two crèmes brûlées, please."

"A bottle just for us? Don't you think it's a bit too much?" I ask.

"Nothing is too much when you are in Paris with a charming Parisienne like you," he says with a sweet smile.

He looks excited, like a teenager. He is not Mister CEO anymore; he is becoming who he really is inside: Erik.

Our desserts arrive. I break the caramel crust of the crème brûlée with my spoon and put a spoonful of the vanilla cream in my mouth. It is smooth, warm, soft and crusty all at once. "Mmm. It's delicious. It melts on the tongue. You really made a good choice, Monsieur."

He smiles, and takes my glass and fills it with Champagne.

"I want to show you this." I take a book from my bag, open it, and show him the poem, "The Love Poem." "It's from Apollinaire, the friend of Picasso. Do you remember? Guillaume Apollinaire?"

"The prince of poets."

"Yes! But Apollinaire was not a very lucky prince in love. By the way, he used to be a good chef, too. He loved women and good food. He wrote famous erotic poems, too. His most famous lover was Marie Laurencin, the female painter. But he suffered a lot with women. Thanks to his heartbreak, he wrote beautiful love poems. Like crème brûlée is your favorite dessert, this poem is my favorite poem. It's not erotic. Sorry to disappoint you."

"Oh no, it's fine. I'm looking forward to learning about the favorite poem of my favorite guide and favorite French teacher."

I blush. The Champagne, the heat of the café, him…I am feeling dizzy. It is hard to focus on Apollinaire. "You see, this poem is very well known in France. All the children learn it at school. It's about a bridge in Paris, 'The Mirabeau Bridge.'"

"Who is Mirabeau? He's Marivaux's cousin?"

"You're right. They have almost the same name. But no. Mirabeau used to be a leader from the French Revolution. Again, the18th century. This poem is moving because Apollinaire is sincere. His words are simple, easy to understand. You can feel how much Apollinaire loved and cried. He is on the bridge. He is sad because his lover does not love him anymore. So, he compares his love with the water of the Seine River. He tells us about time, which goes on like the water, the time that won't come back, the love that won't come back. He tells us how expectation is violent."

I finish my Champagne, place the glass back on the table, and sigh,

"Yes, expectation can be violent, he is right," I say. "Ultimately, things don't change, you know? Les Précieuses from the 17th century, Marivaux from the 18th century, or Apollinaire from the 20th century. They tell us exactly the same thing in their own words. Time, eras, centuries change, yes. We think we are so far from those centuries, but human feelings are still the same. We think we are more modern than them, but we're not. Because feelings don't change. We love and we suffer because of love, like they did before us. We, the very modern people with our wonderful technology."

"Maybe, you know I don't have an artichoke heart because I don't believe in love," he says. "Sorry, I have a stone heart. But please, read on." He drinks his Champagne. "I'm curious to learn what your mister Apollinaire says about love."

Suddenly, my heart drops. If he tells me he has a heart made of stone, that he doesn't believe in love, then his message is very clear: Don't even think I can fall in love with you. Go away! Keep your distance. Who do you think you are? You're wasting your time with me, stupid woman!

He fills my empty glass with Champagne. Is he trying to get me drunk? I am becoming exasperated. The prince of the poets was right. Yes, expectation is violent. I feel foolish. Here I am hoping for something that will never happen. But, why all this? The restaurant? The Champagne? The night in Paris? Is he playing with me? Is he cruel? Anyway, I have to keep my dignity. So, I drink my glass of Champagne for strength, to forget the lump in my throat. I also drink the Champagne because I do like it. It's light, sparkling, and joyful. Exactly like the life I want to live. If only I could have a Champagne life. I clear my throat and read the poem without looking at him:

Le Pont Mirabeau

Sous le pont Mirabeau coule la Seine

Et nos amours

Faut-il qu'il m'en souvienne

La joie venait toujours après la peine

Vienne la nuit sonne l'heure

Les jours s'en vont je demeure

Les mains dans les mains restons face à face

Tandis que sous

Le pont de nos bras passe

Des éternels regards l'onde si lasse

Vienne la nuit sonne l'heure

Les jours s'en vont je demeure

L'amour s'en va comme cette eau courante

L'amour s'en va

Comme la vie est lente

Et comme l'Espérance est violente

Vienne la nuit sonne l'heure

Les jours s'en vont je demeure

Passent les jours et passent les semaines

Ni temps passé
Ni les amours reviennent
Sous le pont Mirabeau coule la Seine
Vienne la nuit sonne l'heure
Les jours s'en vont je demeure
—Guillaume Apollinaire (1880-1918)

The Mirabeau Bridge
Under The Mirabeau Bridge flows the Seine
And lovers
Must I be reminded
Joy came always after pain
The night is a clock chiming
The days go by not I
We're face to face and hand in hand
While under the bridges
Of embrace expire
Eternal tired tidal eyes
The night is a clock chiming
The days go by not I
Love elapses like the river
Love goes by
Poor life is indolent
And expectation always violent
The night is a clock chiming
The days go by not I
The days and equally the weeks elapse
The past remains the past
Love remains lost
Under Mirabeau Bridge the river slips away
The night is a clock chiming
The days go by not I

He does not say a word. Then, he takes something from his coat and puts a packet on the table. It is wrapped with elegant black paper and a Sephora sticker.

"This is for you, young lady."

I am surprised to receive a present from him. I really don't understand. Why did he buy me a present if he doesn't have feelings for me? Oh, of course. I'm so stupid! This is my tip.

"Thanks," I say. "I have a question for you. Why do you always call me 'young lady'?"

"Because you are a young lady. Much younger than me. It's also a compliment because you are a lady"

"I'm not so young, you know. I'm almost 50." My subtext was: Don't even think I'm too young for you, because I'm not. I'm perfect for you.

"No! I don't believe it," he says. "Are you joking? You look no older than forty. Like a kid! How do you do it?"

"You're very nice," I say, "but you're exaggerating a little bit." I laugh. After crying inside, now I am laughing. Blame it on the Champagne. "Well, how much will you pay for my little secrets?"

He smiles back at me. He is so irresistible when he smiles.

"Alright, let's see what it is." I open the square packet. Habanita! My perfume. I thank him profusely. "You shouldn't have!"

"I really liked your French classes. I learned so much thanks to you. So, I wanted to thank you in my own way."

Exactly what I thought. He is just being polite. A cold and polite man. He did not want to give me money as a tip, so he bought my perfume.

But I'm not ungrateful. Indeed, it's an elegant and refined way to thank his teacher. He offered me my favorite perfume, after all. He can't be so cruel. It's not like he's been mean; he chose the most expensive version: the largest bottle that costs a minimum of 150 euros. I open the bottle, put some on my neck and then some on my wrists. Pshhht! Pshht! A vanilla cloud falls around me.

"It smells great. And it suits you," he said. "Vintage and elegant. Like you."

I love the Art Deco design of the bottle, by Lalique, almost as much as I love the scent inside.

"Habanita by Molinard, made in Paris in 1921," he says. "You see, I remember what you told me. It's interesting how you have your own universe. Even with perfume, I learnt something about Paris. That's why I like Paris. It's another world, too. You're so Parisian."

"Me?" I don't feel at all like the stereotypical chic Parisian. I'm just a working-class girl from Belleville."

I see the time. "Oh! It's already half past eleven. Sorry, but I have to go. I don't like to take the Métro late. And I feel very woozy."

"Have some water." He takes his empty glass, because mine still has Champagne, and fills it with water, hands it to me. "I'm so sorry. Are you okay? Do you want to go home? I can pay for a taxi to take you home."

"Oh, thanks." I drink some water. "I feel better now, thank you. No, I don't have to go. I'm fine now."

"Good! I'm happy you're okay. So, let's go. I have an idea."

"Where are we going?"

"It's a surprise, young lady."

Outside the café, the rain has stopped. He looks for a taxi but there are none, so we walk along Boulevard Saint-Germain. I am drunk, and when I'm drunk, I feel happy and less shy. (I should drink more, maybe.)

"Do you know the song about Saint-Germain-des-Prés?" I ask. "'Il n'y a plus d'après' which means 'There is no ever after left.'"

"No, sorry miss," he confesses. "I'm not a great singer but I do like French songs."

"Juliette Greco is the singer. I worship her. She used to be the muse of Sartre and Existentialists in the fifties. She was really a free woman, a rebellious Parisian. Daryl Zanuck the American producer was madly in love with her. They had an affair. But she didn't care about his fame or money. She cared about her freedom. She also was madly in love with Miles Davis."

"The jazz trumpetist?"

"Yes. She talked about how wonderful their love story was here, in Paris, in Saint-Germain-des-Prés. And how difficult it became when they went to Miles Davis's country. In the U.S., she could not travel openly with him. They had to hide, because in the 'fifties in America, a white woman could not love and be loved by a black man, even if he was a famous and talented musician. She was horrified. Juliette Greco was part of the Resistance during WWII, you know. A free mind. They were so in love."

My brain is foggy. I try to remember the song and start to sing.

"Il n'y a plus d'après, à Saint-Germain-des-Prés, plus d'après demain, plus d'après midi il n'y a qu'aujourd'hui...quand je te reverrai à Saint-Germain-des-Prés, ce ne sera plus toi, ce ne sera plus moi, il n'y a plus d'autrefois." "There is no ever after left in Saint-Germain-des-Prés, no day after tomorrow, no more afternoon, there is just today. When I'll see you again, in Saint-Germain-des-Prés, it will no longer be you, it will no longer be me, the old days are gone."

He watches me with an enigmatic smile. "I like this song! I didn't know you were a singer, too. You have a nice voice. You're so Parisian. For me, you are Paris!"

This is the first time I ever heard something like that. That I was Paris to someone. He is probably also buzzed like me.

"Me? Paris? You're funny! But why?"

"I don't know. I can't explain. For me, you are Paris. Voilà. Vous êtes Paris!"

Still no taxi. Suddenly, he whistles, and a taxi stops. This man is so funny!

"I never thought you could whistle like that," I tell him, winking.

He opens the taxi door. "Madame, please."

I go inside while he goes around to the driver's door and tells him something I can't hear. Then, he joins me. And it inundates me: his strong scent. I know this scent, a strong lavender. Of course! Pour un Homme by Caron. The one I mentioned to him. My favorite men's cologne. If he bought this cologne that I like so much, it must have been intended to please me.

"Your perfume is Pour un Homme?" I ask.

"Yes." He looks like a little boy caught taking a cookie from the jar. It is so adorable.

The taxi's radio plays jazz. The music stops and a woman's sensual voice comes on. "You are listening to FIP, radio for Parisians who don't sleep. In fifteen minutes, it will be midnight."

For once, I don't say a word. I have nothing to say. I am just enjoying the moment: sitting beside him, smelling his magical cologne, admiring the dreamy view from our taxi, and listening to jazz. We pass the most beautiful bridge in Paris, the bridge named for the Russian tsar, Alexandre III. It is shining.

We drive along the Seine, pass many bridges. But where are we going? On a Seine cruise? So late?

"Surprise, Madame!" He turns to me, smiles and places his finger on his lips. "Shhhhhh."

I wish he would at least take my hand. I wish he would take more risks. Why doesn't he take my face between his delicate fingers and kiss me softly in this taxi? No. He does absolutely nothing. He is still. He does not speak. He does not move. So, I do not say anything, either. Maybe it is his Scandinavian education? Maybe he is too shy to do or say something romantic?

We pass a red café with white letters on the front. Because it is dark, I can hardly read what they say. But then:

"Oh! Café Apollinaire!" I say, realizing. "Too funny. We talked about his poem and now here we are. What a strange coincidence."

The taxi stops and he pays the driver. I see that he slipped him a huge tip. This man is very generous. With everybody. He has a good heart. I want to open my door to exit the cab, but he insists, "No, please wait, Madame." He jumps out of the taxi, opening my door like a gentleman.

I recognize the bridge: Mirabeau Bridge! Of course! It was not a coincidence. No wonder he wanted it to be a surprise. The bridge in "The Love Poem." So, he was moved by Apollinaire's poem.

As we walk on the bridge, it starts to rain again. It is dark with very little light. He opens his big umbrella with one hand, takes my waist with the other, and pulls me close. "I don't want you to get wet," he whispers in my ear, softly. We can hardly see each other. Then, he holds me tight. He whispers again with a warm, sweet voice. "You touched my heart, young lady."

I smile and put my head on his shoulder. We stay silent, tight under the umbrella, listening to the sound of the rain falling around us. I take his hand in mine and I show him the view of the Eiffel Tower from our bridge.

"It will be midnight in one minute! Look, Erik!"

"I like when you call me Erik with your French accent. It sounds so soft."

That minute, the Eiffel tower lights up and sparkles just for us...the two lovers on the bridge. In that moment, everything mixes together: the water from the sky with the water from the Seine; the shining Eiffel Tower with the dark Mirabeau Bridge; the prince of the poets with the queen of Egypt; his lavender with my vanilla; la Précieuse with Pierre de Marivaux; the serious Swede with the Romantic French woman; his stone heart with my marshmallow heart.

Chapter 7:

The Cheeky Frog at the American Library

FOR A LONG TIME, I WAS CONVINCED THAT I HAD AN ENGLISH accent. I was glad because I do love an English accent. It's elegant and chic. I remember my first English class—three times a week we had an English lesson with Mr. Bolton, our nice English teacher from Manchester. We watched a VHS video tape about the fabulous life of the Brown family in London, on the BBC. Since I mentioned it was a VHS, you can imagine it was in the very beginning of the '80s.

We had to repeat again and again, "Where is Brian? Brian is in the kitchen. What are Mrs. Brown and Brian Brown doing? Mrs. Brown is having a cup of tea. Brian Brown is drinking a glass of water." Everyone had an English accent: Mr. Bolton, the speaker from the BBC, and the Brown family.

Learning English, for me, was a window on a new world. At 12 years of age, I was discovering a new language and culture. For five years, I was happy to learn English in middle school then in high school. My English teachers were not always British, but they all had a perfect English accent.

Then, much later, I met John. John, who was from the north of England, was living in Paris with Miranda, his friendly American girlfriend. He was proud to have studied at Oxford. I would be proud, too, if I had studied at this historic, prestigious English university. John made me realize that I was not speaking English with an English accent, shattering my illusions.

When I was looking for a job, a travel agent from New York, who lives in Paris, told me she would never hire me as a tour guide. When I asked her why, she said, "Because my American clients would never understand you with your French accent." I felt offended, but what could I do? Nothing, I guess. I had to accept the awful truth: I never had and will never have an English accent when I speak English.

The relationship between England and France is like a couple. Love and hate. Fascination and repulsion. The English and French are both fascinated by each other's culture and history, but from time to time they can't bear each other. We sometimes hate England because of our mutual history. They invaded us in the Middle Ages. We were at war against the English for more than a hundred years—a hundred and sixteen years to be precise. That's a lot.

An Indian friend of mine once asked me who invaded whom exactly? My answer was simple: "Would you invade a country where it's always raining, the food is boiled, and Champagne doesn't exist?" Voilà. England invaded France.

And I'm not even mentioning Joan of Arc, Louis the XIV, and Napoleon, who were not very fond of the English. Why did the French give gunpowder, guns, and their best generals to help Les Insurgés (rebel colonists) during the American Revolution? Insurgés was the name given by the French to the future Americans. Because we had a common enemy: the English.

England and France are like husband and wife, but France and the U.S. are more like brother and sister. France does not always agree with the U.S. They fight, argue, and shout sometimes. But they are still brother and sister. Two Republics. If one of the republics is suffering, or in danger, we help each other, like a real family. If you go to Normandy, you'll see written in English on the shop windows, "Welcome to our liberators." The first time I went to the American cemetery in Normandy, I cried reading the ages on the many graves of American soldiers who fell on French beaches during D-Day in August 1944. They were all so young.

But even with your best enemy, you must make peace one day. So, in 1904 L'Entente Cordiale (The Agreement of Cordiality) was signed between the U.K. and France., thanks to Edward, Prince of Wales, who was called "The Peacemaker" and was very much a Francophile. Edward VII was the exact opposite of his puritanical mother, Queen Victoria. He loved France, the Parisian lifestyle, and more than anything else, sensual French women. Cherchez la femme. He even had his own chaise des voluptés in his favorite Parisian brothel, which enabled him to have sex with two women at the same time. This chair was designed for him because "Dirty Bertie," as his compatriots called him, liked French food as much as he liked French women, so he was overweight and needed a bit of help to enjoy the delights of love.

Do you know what the French call an English education? It's a masochist relationship that men, English or not, could find in the famous Parisian brothels. In the Belle Epoque, Paris was the brothel capital of the world—but refined brothels with elegant rooms, glamorous courtesans, cultured music, and Champagne, of course. It was not glamorous for everyone, though. There also were sordid brothels where women had to turn 50 tricks a day.

I worry I'm spoiling the mood, so let's talk about how the French were also obsessed with the English in the 19th century—their own Anglomania. Everything that was English was in fashion: the language, clubs, clothes, literature. English tea, English food—oh no, not English food. Never English food.

The English also had their French follie (madness). You know the expression, "Excuse my French?" You might think it's when someone says a vulgar word in English, but haven't you wondered why they say this when no one had said even one word of French? Because it doesn't mean what you think it does. In the 19th century, it was very fashionable for the English to sprinkle French words in their sentences. But as the English are very polite, they'd apologize for their bad French. "He had that je ne sais quoi about him. Oh, excuse my French, my dear."

The English people are famous for being very funny. So, of course, I find my friend John hilarious. He has that typical dry English humor: self-deprecating and very ironic. When I laugh, he asks me with his refined English accent from Oxford, "But why do you laugh?"

"You are so funny!"

"No, I'm not. Stop laughing please."

The English call the French, "Frogs." It's ugly as a frog. And I never eat frog's legs, anyway. We call the English Les Roastbeefs because the English supposedly sunburn easily with their fair skin, red as English beef. Roast beef is not a very elegant name, either. John is always elegant, and he's never red from the sun. He naturally tans. John does not need designer clothes to create his own style. Sometimes, John wears saffron-colored jeans with a yellow jacket and brown shoes. But he can also wear a striped, black shirt with a plum-colored velvet jacket without looking ridiculous. On the contrary, he is extremely stylish. Like most English men, John is not afraid to be audacious when it's a question of style.

But what John is best at (best, except for his sartorial style and his humor) are his parties. Each month, he invites people to his fantastic Parisian apartment. Everybody brings something to eat. He calls it his "Potluck Party." He invites many different kinds of people, so it's always a fun mix: Bourgeois and Bohemians, Parisians and tourists, Americans and Russians, French Frogs and English Roastbeefs. The problem is that John never asks his guests what they are going to bring. So sometimes we have to share a lot of cheese because everybody brings cheese. Then John has to run in the rain to find a bakery open at 9 o'clock in the evening to buy bread to eat with all that cheese. Or sometimes we have only cakes to eat because everybody's brought desserts.

When I ask John why he doesn't check to see what his guests are bringing, he responds, "But why? That's the charm of my party. We don't know who'll be there, what we'll eat—and sometimes we don't even know if we'll eat."

The English are a bit eccentric and that's why I like them. John's parties are super popular, and I always have fun with the friendly people I meet. But sometimes, I must confess, I have major problems with l'anglais. I mean the language, not the exquisite people from the big island.

During one of his potluck parties, John told me, "Did you hear how you spoke to this poor American gentleman? I really felt sorry for him. You were not very nice."

"What?"

"You don't say 'What?' my dear," he said. "It's not polite. You say, 'Excuse me, I beg your pardon, or 'sorry."

"I'm sorry, your Majesty, but could your Royal Highness please repeat?" I rebuffed. "I did not say anything unfriendly to this American!"

"Oh, really?" John said. "When he told you he was an expert in 19th century French, you asked him if he had a PhD, or at least a license. When he answered that he did not, you said—"

"Oh, yes," I interjected. "I remember. I told him that for the French, you are only an 'expert' if you have a PhD or at least a license in the subject you purport to master. Writing books or articles on a blog about 19th century French, even if they are very interesting, does not make you an expert. You can say, 'I like 19th century French' or 'I have an interest or a passion for the 19th century.' So yes, I told him he did not have the credentials to be an expert in 19th century France. Sorry."

"It was not very friendly to make fun of him."

"I was not unfriendly at all!" I said. "I just told him the truth. I'm sorry if I'm outspoken. And in the end, he thanked me for teaching him how to behave in Parisian society. We laughed a lot."

"If I was telling half of what you say to Americans, Americans would slap me," John said. "But you, with your funny French way of speaking

English, you make Americans laugh. They are never angry with you. You're a cheeky French girl."

"Excuse me, your Majesty, now it's you who is not being very polite. I thought Englishmen were gentlemen."

"Me? But what did I say?"

"What did you say? I know I have big cheeks! It's no reason to call me a 'cheeky' French girl."

John smiled. "Not cheeky as in your cheeks. You don't have big cheeks! Cheeky means effrontée, in French. Insolent. Insolente."

John's smile widened into a big grin. Alright, so I misunderstand English words, sometimes. Well, quite often to be honest. Plus, there are some English words that I cannot properly pronounce. Once, I did a guided visit for a woman from Kansas. She was quite rude to me. I was very angry with her, so when I joined Miranda (John's girlfriend) for a coffee after my visit, I told her all that happened.

"We were in the Louvre, and she was criticizing and complaining all the time—a real bossy, spoiled princess. She demanded I make an extra visit to the Da Vinci exhibition, which was full. She demanded I make a visit to the Egyptian section, which was not included in the visit. She demanded I stay longer with her because she was afraid to walk 50 meters alone in Paris to join her friends at a restaurant. I tried to be as nice as I could. Well, I just learned that this beach complained about me!" I was furious. Miranda started to laugh "You mean she is a bitch! Ah! You are too funny!"

And I can't pronounce the "th" sound either, which is highly inconvenient when your name is Edith. So, Anglophones don't understand when I introduce myself. And I end up feeling ridiculous.

I do my best to speak English well, but it's not easy. I don't have a license for English. I never studied English at the university level; I only studied English from age 12 to 17. That's it. My father is not Canadian, my mother is not Welsh, my family never moved to Australia when I was a teenager, and I never spent a year in London or New York, or even six months in Ireland. I honed my English on my own, in Paris. I'm a self-made woman of English. And I'm proud to be able to speak English, even if my English is far from perfect—and even if my pronunciation sometimes sounds weird.

But I have one regret in life about English: it's that I have been unable to read the original version of Pride and Prejudice. Unfortunately, my English is too weak to read this brilliant Jane Austen book. Of course, I've read it in French, and I watched the BBC series. I don't mean the movie with Keira Knightley; I mean the 1995 series with the seductive British actor Colin Firth as Darcy.

One afternoon, I was invited for tea by Miranda and John along with Phoebe, a British expat. I was helping John prepare the tea in the kitchen, and he passed to me teacups with the Union Jack imprinted on them. Then he put the Scottish shortbread on a plate that was decorated with a portrait of Princess Diana.

Inspired by this British mood, I declared, "It is a truth universally acknowledged that a single man in possession of a good fortune must be in want of a wife."

John looked at me as if I were crazy. "What's the matter with you?" he said. "I don't have money and I'm not single. And anyway, I don't want a wife. Do you want to marry a rich single man? And what a strange way to speak English! Is it Shakespeare?"

"Not at all!" I told him, munching on some shortbread. "It's the first sentence of "Pride and Prejudice." I know it by heart. Haven't you read it?"

He hadn't. "But Miranda has. At Oxford. We make fun of Jane Austen fans. It's really girl stuff! British men don't read Jane Austen. Only women." He called it "chick lit" and said it wasn't on his level.

I insisted he read it. "I envy you and Miranda because you can read Jane Austen in English. It's a really great book. It doesn't matter if it's a woman's book or a man's book. 'Pride and Prejudice' is definitely not chick lit!"

I suppose I convinced John, because he finally acquiesced. "But I won't buy it," he said. "I don't want to take the risk. I'll borrow it from the American Library."

A few weeks later, Miranda, John, Phoebe, and I were sipping our English tea and eating chocolate digestive biscuits in front of the TV. John loved the book "Pride and Prejudice" so much that he also borrowed the DVD of the BBC series from the American library of Paris. And for the 5th time, I was charmed by the delightful characters of Jane Austen.

I had no idea there was an American Library in Paris. And it's not a small one. The American library is the biggest English-language lending library outside the U.S. on the continent.

It was created when American writer Edith Wharton was living in Paris in the 19th century, when the community of American expats was the biggest in Europe. Of course, it was John and Miranda who took me there for the first time. I love this place. I love all the books. Many literary events are organized there with smart American writers, and sometimes British and even French come to the prestigious American Library of Paris to lecture about their books.

John called me one day about an event at the library. "I don't know who's coming but the book is about French women, written by an American. Miranda wants to go. She's read all those books written by Americans about French women. Believe me there are a lot. Do you want to join us? It's next Saturday"

"Eh. I don't know."

"You should! I'm sure American women will be interested to hear what a cheeky French woman like you has to say."

• • •

There are a lot of people, at least a hundred. All the seats in the American library are taken, mostly by American women. I spot a hand waving. Oh! It's John! Great! He kept a seat for me.

"Where is Miranda?" I ask.

"She couldn't attend. Her family from Boston is in town," he says. "Please sit! It's going to start."

A young man talks into the microphone. He is the moderator of the lecture. He introduces a chic, blond American writer in her late fifties, from New York. Then he shows the blue cover of her book; pink letters said: "Ooh la la: French Women's Secrets to Feeling Beautiful Every Day." Then Jamie Cat Callan, the American author, explains to us in a lively way how much she likes French women. She ends her lecture by reading an excerpt of her book.

Miss Jamie is quite amusing. She has a sweet and musical voice; it reminds me a bit of Marilyn Monroe's voice. I love Marilyn Monroe. Indeed, John was right. There are dozens of books written in English about French women. It is lovely to hear the charming Jamie telling us how wonderful French women are: always elegant, always sexy, always refined.

I am flattered, of course, but also a bit annoyed. When the moderator asks for questions, everyone agrees that French women are perfect models for other women. Everybody, that is, except me.

I want to speak. I shoot up out of my chair.

"What are you doing?" asks John, trepidation in his voice. "Please don't forget I belong to this honored community." He cringes. "I'm well known here. Please be nice!"

The moderator makes a sign to give me the floor.

John puts his hand in front of his face and whispers to me with his sexy English accent, "Oh. My. God."

I whisper back. "John, don't be scared. You know that I'm always nice!"

I am nervous to speak in front of so many educated Anglophones in my terrible English. So, I take a deep breath for courage. I know that they are not going to like what I am about to say.

"Good evening," I start. "I don't have any questions but a comment. I'm annoyed by all these books about French and Parisian women that say that French women are perfect. As you can tell from my accent, I'm a French woman, and if I believe most of these books as a French woman, I don't get fat, I am always chic, I am a femme fatale with many lovers and I am also the best mother in the world!

"You know what?" I say smiling, "it's a little too much for one woman—even for me! I feel very sorry for my American sisters. And if I were an American woman, I would hate French women! But you'll notice that the hundreds of books and articles about the myth of the French woman have all been written by American women, not French. French women would not be so arrogant as to pretend to teach other women in the world how to behave. All those books are only about marketing and sales."

Finished with my "lecture," I sit back down. I can feel my face flushed from speaking publicly, and because of my emotion.

John turns to me with a smile. "Well said, cheeky girl."

I thought the American women in the salon would be angered by my comments. But the reaction was not what I was expecting. After the lecture, dozens of American women from different ages came up to me to thank me. They said they were relieved to hear a French woman say what I'd said. It took the weight off them to be perfect like a French woman.

"Reject it!" I told these women. "You don't have to be a French woman. What's wrong with being an American woman? You're already great. I reject this concept of telling American women that there is something wrong with them, that they have to be like French women just to sell books. It's not reality, it's marketing. I don't like that American women should feel bad about themselves. Not in my name!"

But I wasn't at ease with my public intervention. I had to express myself, but I felt sorry for Jamie, the charming American writer. She was so gracious, and I was so aggressive. I had to apologize to her.

I thought she would be angry, but her behavior surprised me. When I approached her, she was signing a copy of her book. She looked up at me with a warm smile. We started chatting about those books dedicated to French women.

"Jamie, there is something I don't understand. Why do you want to become French? If you were French, like me, you would have attacked me for calling you out in front of your audience, but you smiled at me. I'm impressed by your behavior. To me, you represent everything good about American women: Smiling, friendly, enthusiastic, self-confident, and open-minded. Do you really want to become pessimistic, arrogant, and grumpy... like me?"

She laughs, telling me I was funny—and so French. She explains that she is not trying to become a French woman because she is happy to be American. It is about gaining inspiration from French women, to find her inner femininity and her joy of life. She adds that French women feel like big sisters to American women.

I'd never thought about this idea. How interesting! It reminded me of what another American author wrote, Francophile Edith Wharton. She said that Americans are teenagers while French are adults.

Before leaving the American library, Jamie and I exchange emails, promising to keep in touch, and grab a coffee in Paris.

On my way home from the American Library, as I was walking through the elegant, quiet streets of the 7th arrondissement of Paris, I started thinking: Alright, so we are the big sisters of American women. Like big sisters, we French women give our tips to feel better in their lives. So, the relationship between French women and American women was not as condescending as I had thought. It is kind. And why not?

Suddenly a question sprang to mind: If French women inspire American women, who inspires French women? And what about the mythical Parisienne? Who inspires her?

Chapter 8:

Do It Like a Parisienne!

THE FAMOUS IMAGE OF THE PARISIAN WOMAN IS BOTH CULtural and historical. It's during the 17th and 18th centuries that the French developed an aesthetic conscience, not only in art and in architecture, but also in daily life. And this vivid concept of aestheticism explains why modern Parisian women are still aware that being elegant is key to their life.

Everything started during Le Grand Siècle. The Great Century was the glorious era of the French King Louis XIV. During the 17th century, France had the most talented architects, interior designers, landscape gardeners (like André Le Nôtre), writers, and philosophers (like Molière, Pierre Corneille, Jean de La Fontaine, Jean Racine, René Descartes, etc.). Thanks to the influence of the brilliant Sun King Louis XIV, and his genius super-Minister Jean-Baptiste Colbert, France became the European model of good taste. The marvelous castle of Versailles, a symbol of the glory for France, was replicated 28 times in Europe (not all the copies were completed). The European elite wanted to speak French and dress like French aristocrats. France was the arbiter of Western good taste, and all of Europe wanted French products.

Being refined in the 17th century meant to be elegant. The court of Versailles became a permanent theater where one had to always present oneself. The same theater still exists for the French on the streets of Paris: the terraces of Paris cafés have replaced the court of Versailles. That's why in Paris, café chairs face the street! You watch and you are watched.

Show must go on, and being elegant means fashion. So, the French developed their passion for fashion. No surprise that the first fashion magazine, Le Mercure Galant, debuted in Paris in 1672. This periodical was more popular in Europe than Vogue or Harper's Bazaar is today. If you glance at the sophisticated French ladies in Le Mercure Galant, you will notice that the French woman of the Great Century was not only a fashion victim, but was also slim.

Then along came the Age of Enlightenment in the 18th century. French women, such as Madame Geoffrin and Madame du Deffand, created the fashionable literary salons in Paris. In these intellectual salons, great philosophers including Voltaire, Denis Diderot, and Jean d'Alembert could debate freely, and criticize the royal power. Outspoken Parisian women broadcast the Enlightenment's ideas, which became the basis of the French Revolution.

During this century, Scottish philosopher David Hume lived in Paris for many years. The French warmly welcomed him, and he came to know and love France. Hume wrote that the English are better philosophers than the French, just as the Italians are better musicians and painters than the French. But he said the French are the only ones in the world who bring to life the subtlest and most agreeable art: the art of living (l'art de vivre). Hume explained that the art of living is the pleasure of talking and of showing oneself.

One afternoon, I was strolling in the Orsay museum among the Impressionist paintings, when I suddenly understood something: before the invention of photography in the 19th century, there were the French Impressionists. And how to capture an image of the refined Parisienne? By the paintings. Claude Monet, Auguste Renoir, and Edgar Degas painted the elegant Parisian woman from the French bourgeoisie. One can admire her, wearing a glamorous dress from the first haute-couture designer, the British (but very Parisian) Worth. The Impressionists also represented the fresh and happy working-class Parisian woman, who had fun on the weekend along the River Seine. Renoir painted again and again the sensual Parisian woman. La Parisienne also fascinated Edouard Manet. He painted many alluring, proud Parisian women. Thanks to this talent, we discover on a painting a beautiful hat, the delicate multi-colored fabric of a silk dress, shining gloves, and ribbons. And of course, Manet suggests the very tight corset of this elegant woman who has a tiny, sexy waist. If you admire the paintings by Manet, like La femme au Perroquet (1868), La femme au Balcon (1868), and Le chemin de fer (1873), you will immediately understand how French painters from the 19th century, even now, still promote the myth of the chic Parisienne all over the world.

What French painters did with their paintings, French writers did with their words. The hero of Emile Zola's novels, Octave Mouret, has a unique goal in life: to conquer the Parisienne. Zola wrote: "The Parisian woman is a tourist attraction, every bit as much as the Eiffel Tower." (Pot-Bouille, 1882).

And who could forget the incredible Parisian aristocrat of the Belle Époque, the very chic, snobbish, and beautiful Oriane, duchesse de Guermantes, described so well by Marcel Proust in his book "In Search of Lost Time?" The model for this fascinating woman was the very Parisian, refined, and eccentric Comtesse de Greffulhe, who mesmerized Proust. Her inimitable style and personality also inspired the best haute-couture designers in Paris. She remains so relevant that in 2015, the fashion museum of Paris, Le Palais Galliera, organized a popular exhibition just about her, which I saw twice.

There are also many inspirational Parisian women from the 20th century: The Roaring Twenties and its mythical Parisians. Coco Chanel, who created the little black dress, and set women free with her revolutionary designs and modern clothes. Kiki de Montparnasse, the charismatic muse of the top artists of the '20s. Then, in the 1950s, the feminist Simone de Beauvoir. Those women became the symbol of the free Parisienne who chooses her life—and her loves.

The Parisian woman is outspoken. She can be cheeky and rebellious, like the singers Edith Piaf and Juliette Greco. She can be bourgeois and conservative like the actresses Catherine Deneuve and Fanny Ardant. In the 1960s, the blond Brigitte Bardot and the brunette Jeanne Moreau, created the image of the French woman full of charm, sex appeal, and personality. What do those Parisian women have in common? L'esprit—spirit. La Parisienne is witty, lively, and hates the idea of perfection, because perfection is boring. So instead of trying to be perfect, the Parisian woman expresses her own personality.

• • •

How to find your unique fashion style? Do it like Coco Chanel.

Paul Morand, the French writer and intimate friend of Coco Chanel, said, "Chanel built her fashion as one builds a hut." He meant that Coco Chanel created modern clothes to suit herself, not all women. She made her own style for her own body. We sometimes forget that she was born in 1883, in the Belle Epoque, when a woman had to be curvaceous, and overly adorned with baubles and lace. Chanel said that she did not have the curvaceous body type for all this feminine frippery. So, she found her own style. She created a boyish style, using the men's suits: The man's white shirt, the black tie, the jockey jacket, naval jerseys, Jodhpurs, and of course, the cropped, trimmed Austrian men's jacket she adapted for her celebrated suit from the '60s.

Do like Chanel: Don't follow fashion trends; choose clothes that suit your body shape and your own taste. Chanel said, "I chose what I wanted to be."

One day, I also chose what I wanted to be.

Everything started in my car. Before I used to wear large skirts, large dark tops and Birkenstock sandals. Birkenstocks are very comfortable, but not exactly Louboutin. I looked like a hippie. It was easy and convenient— and what's wrong looking like a hippie? But one day, while driving in my car, I saw a huge billboard for Les 3 Suisses, a French mail order business, since 1955. It's not really a trendy brand, but I liked the image: a brunette wearing a black striped shirt with a red pencil skirt. The look was accessorized with a thick, black belt and stacks of chunky, red bangles on both wrists. You'll agree, this was not at all my "hippie from Kathmandu" style.

But something happened inside me when I saw this ad. More than the clothes, I was mesmerized by the attitude of the model. She didn't have a big smile as most models do in ads. It was more of a half-smile, and she had her hands on her hips. Her expression and body language said, "This is who I am! I'm a playful woman because life is a play!" Suddenly, the words of the song by KT Tunstall popped into my head. Do you remember this song? "Suddenly I see, this is what I want to be!" Me, too, I suddenly wanted to be like the model in the ad. I wanted to wear a black striped shirt with a red pencil skirt. I wanted to be cute, to feel like a woman and to have fun exactly like her. I wanted to be playful, with a life that sparkles like Champagne.

I'm not so naive that I was unaware I fell into a marketing trap. I suppose this was the goal of this ad: to make me buy the clothes. But it was the first time I had this reaction. I'm never normally influenced by fashion ads. I was just grabbed by a sudden jolt of inspiration on this day. I realized I had found my personal style!

When I arrived home, I immediately bought the clothes in the ad, including the black belt and red bangles. And my life changed. I stopped hiding my pathetic divorcee's grief behind black, long skirts and large dark tops. I had been a depressed single mom, no men to love me. But I decided that if nobody was loving me, I had to love myself. I decided that I deserved to wear better clothes. I exchanged my shapeless, sad, black clothes for bright red pencil skirts, polka dots dresses, and striped tops.

From invisible to visible.

• • •

Everyone is an artist. Just be an audacious woman. Chanel said elegance is refusal. It means refusing to imitate the others. Be artful. Your style is your way of expressing your personality to the world. It is your personal way of putting poetry in your prosaic, daily routine. Style is a way to make your day more elegant, and happier, too. You deserve to wear clothes you like. Have you seen the people in the Métro? Everybody wears blue jeans. Yuck! It's so boring! But I'm not going to tell you how to dress like a Parisian woman because I'm not a fashion expert. There are excellent books out there already, written by fashion gurus who can give you good advice. What's important is to be creative.

My friend Madeleine is a tour guide in Paris. She's funny, good looking Parisienne in her fifties, with auburn hair and green eyes. Madeleine has one passion in life: Egyptian and Greek History. In summer, she wears dresses inspired by the Ancient Greeks, with many pleats. And she has the same hairstyle you see on statues of Greek women in the Louvre. Sometimes she wears chunky ethnic bracelets on both arms, and black kohl liner framing her green eyes. She becomes a modern and stylish Cleopatra. Madeleine has her own universe, her own style, her own way to express her creativity. She found her inspiration in history. And she doesn't do it to please men (she is successful with men already); she chooses her clothes to please herself to inspire her days. Madeleine is a diva, and people love her because she's interesting. Her clothes reflect her personality; lively and not at all boring.

Great clothes bring self-confidence. I have a good Parisian friend, Louise. She is a slim and cute brunette in her late forties. When she has a stressful meeting, like with her banker or CPA, she wears her best dress and chicest pumps. For her, it's more effective than a Prozac. Louise feels immediately more confident, and it cheers her. Even her banker can't resist her. He is more understanding with her bank overdraft. Yes, clothes can change your mood.

Camille has a charming accent when she speaks French. I call it the "sunny accent." I find it adorable. Camille comes from the South of France—Marseille to be exact—but she's lived in Paris for many years. She looks more like a Norwegian than the typical Mediterranean woman: tall, blond, with beautiful blue eyes. A psychologist, Camille is a warm person, with a strong personality, who likes to laugh and talk. She worships the color white. In summer, she is always in white, and it suits her very well. And in winter she is always in black with pops of color. She'll add a red bracelet or an orange flower on the lapel of her jacket, for example. She took inspiration from the modern paintings of Mondrian, Pollock, Rothko, or of the French modernist painter Yves Klein who, in 1962, developed his own color called International Klein Blue (IKB 191), an electric cobalt blue still used today. Camille's clothes are her way to express her taste, to be as creative as an artist, not just a serious therapist.

Chanel said when you go out, even for five minutes, you should be perfect because you never know if you'll meet the man of your life. I adapted her quotation for my "You never know" rule.

I don't try to be perfect, and I'm not looking for the man of my life, but I still try to look my best—for myself. And you never know what's in store for your day. Life is full of surprises.

• • •

Nineteenth century Romantic Era writer, George Sand, was an incredible woman. I say Romantic Era but it was more so for men than women. France of the 19th century was a very misogynistic time. A French woman could not divorce, could not vote, and could not work without the authorization of her husband. She was treated like a child by society. So, what did George Sand do? She wrote books with a man's pseudonym, hence "George." She became a celebrated female author, and gained a fortune. She was also the first woman to be awarded a legal separation from her husband. (Divorce was forbidden, but separation was not.)

George Sand had many lovers—younger lovers. Polish composer Frederic Chopin, French poet Musset, among many others. She was a free Parisian woman. Her close circle of friends were writers Flaubert and Balzac. Delacroix, the great painter, was her confidant. George Sand also fought for children's rights, and for the poor and uneducated.

What is the link between George Sand and fashion? In 19th century France, it was illegal for women to wear pants. She could do so on only two occasions: riding a horse, or a bicycle. So, a Parisian woman had to ask the police for authorization, and carry with her written proof, or be arrested in the street. Can you imagine asking for authorization every time you want to wear your jeans?

Parisian women had no choice but to wear dresses with tight, painful corsets and squeeze their feet into narrow shoes. Imagine how you would feel at the end of your day if you had to walk in the rain, and with no side-walks back then, that would mean trudging in mud. And don't even think of running to catch the last bus while wearing such constraining and heavy outfits.

Clothes were the prison of French women. Those delicate but inconvenient clothes had a social aim: keeping women at home with her husband and children—keeping them in the private space. In the 19th century, public spaces were for men only. But George Sand did not like to be constrained by this "prison." She wanted to be able to live as men did—to be able to stroll the streets. Une flâneuse—stroller, like George Sand was, found it more convenient to wear men's clothes, and men's supportive shoes to walk in. So, she did just that. She also smoked cigars in public. Shocking! George Sand became the model for all European women who wanted to be free, including the English writer, Charlotte Brontë.

George Sand wore trousers, but not ugly men's trousers. She chose elegant men's clothes. She wore black trousers with a slim fit frock coat. Around her delicate neck, she tied a black silk scarf. On her feet, chic men's leather boots. She looked like a real dandy. Delacroix, her best friend, painted her portrait in her male uniform.

While she wore men's clothes, she was still very feminine. This is how she seduced the debauched Alfred de Musset, star of the Romantic poets. Before Chanel and Yves Saint Laurent, George Sand invented the tuxedo for women.

I'm not like George Sand; I don't wear trousers often, except when it's very cold. But I always have George Sand in mind when I wear them, and I try to be as chic as she used to be. One cold day in January, I had to go to Reims to do a guided tour for an American couple. Reims is in the east of France. It's in the cathedral in Reims where all the French kings were crowned. Reims is also just near the prestigious Champagne vineyards. I do like going to the Champagne district even if it's freezing in winter. I had the thought to wear pants so I wouldn't be cold, but I don't wear jeans since I don't like how they fit me. Instead, under my thick coat, I wore black wool oversized trousers with a white men's shirt. Around my collar, I tied a thick satin ribbon into a large knot. And I topped it off with a navy blue tuxedo jacket. After my guided visit at the beautiful Gothic Cathedral of Reims, I was very cold. Once my visit was finished, I still had plenty of time before my train to Paris, so I decided to buy a book about the Reims district at the tourism office. I chose a comfortable café nearby and sat to read my book while I warmed up. As I was reading "The Incredible Story of Champagne" while sipping a hot chocolate, I felt that someone was staring at me. I wondered if there was something wrong with me, but the person at the table beside me leaned over and said, "Excuse me, but I couldn't help noticing how elegant you look. I wanted to compliment your style, Madame. You remind me of George Sand."

I smiled. He glanced at my book and asked me if I liked the Champagne region. I told him I was a tour guide from Paris; he told me he was an architect from Reims. In the end, I didn't read much of my book. I was too busy talking with this charming architect, all about the history of his incredible city. At the end of our conversation, he gave me his business card and told me with a smile that he came to Paris often for work, and would be happy to continue our conversation over coffee at a café some time.

"In order to be irreplaceable, one must always be different," said Chanel. Indeed, she was right. If I had worn ordinary blue jeans and a warm (but dull) sweater, the cute architect might not have noticed me. So, even in trousers you can be stylish.

But being a Parisienne is not only a question of style and effortless chic; being a Parisian woman is a state of mind. The Parisienne likes to be free. And this Parisian state of mind was shaped by the history of Paris.

Chapter 9:

The Paris Effect

PEOPLE LIKE PARIS BECAUSE IT'S SEEN AS A ROMANTIC CITY. But the history of Paris has not always been so romantic.

Paris was built on violence.

Parisians have always had to fight to protect their city and maintain their liberty, including Parisian women. In January 2015, two million Parisians took to the streets to defend their freedom against the terror attacks. But before 2015, Parisians died many times in the name of freedom. First, the population of Paris had to fight against Viking and English invaders. In 1789, Parisians died in the French Revolution. Then there were the bloody barricades in 1830 and 1848 against dictatorships. In 1870, when Paris was isolated from the rest of France and surrounded by the Prussians, thousands of Parisians died of hunger, cold, and disease. Starving Parisians had to eat rats, cats, and dogs. Then one year later, Paris endured the violent civil war of the Paris Commune, which killed men, women, and children in 1871. And in the 20th century, Parisians endured the world wars, and the invasion of their beloved city by the Nazis.

But what is the link between the bloody history of Paris and the elegant style of the Parisian woman? The Parisian woman is not just the cold image of a fashion plate in high heels. Being Parisian is a way of life, a behavior. The unique, violent, and bloody history of Paris built the soul of the Parisian woman. She is in love with freedom—la liberté. Liberté is the first word engraved on the walls of all French city halls: Liberté, Egalité, Fraternité (Freedom, Equality, Brotherhood). The Parisian woman has a strong personality; she does not care if people like her or not. France is an individualist country. What matters for the French is to express your own personality. To belong to the group, to the community, is less important. That's why you will never see 'the most popular girl' award in a French high school. The French don't care about being popular. They could care less about pleasing everybody.

"To please everyone is to please no one in particular," said writer Sacha Guitry. And what's important for the Parisian woman is to feel free to be herself, not an artificial version of what she should be. This is the mysterious "effortless chic" phenomenon. The French woman is chic, but she does not try too hard. She doesn't make too much of an effort, because she doesn't want to be too perfect. The rejection of perfection. Many American, British, and Australian journalists, writers, and fashion bloggers have tried to decode this "effortless Parisian chic," the idea that you just rolled out of bed looking elegant. Of course, French women make a huge effort (as smart Anglophone fashion experts have discovered) but they will never tell you; they'll pretend it's natural.

But the style doctors forget to tell you that the mysterious "effortless chic" of French women is also cultural. In France, you have to be humble. You never brag, even if you have a PhD. You don't demand that people call you "doctor" unless you are a medical doctor (MD). Otherwise, you seem pedantic and ridiculous. It's the same with "effortless chic." When you have a good meal at a restaurant, do you think the chef will tell you, "Oh, it was so difficult to do! I spent 10 hours in my kitchen!"? Of course not. The same is true with a great pianist. Do you think he or she will explain the 12 hours a day of practice? No. You never tell someone the efforts you made. That which seems easy demands a lot of work.

What you think is chic without effort needs work, too. But it's not polite to show or to talk about the effort to be chic. So, if Parisian women look chic without seemingly making an effort, they will never admit the effort made. But not because she is an arrogant Parisienne, but because she's polite, humble, and discreet. I know, maybe I'm not writing in good faith, but I need to plead for my Parisian sisters from time to time.

I wanted to obtain the opinion of a beauty expert regarding this "effortless chic." On a train from Bordeaux to Paris, I met Bobbi Brown, the creator of the well-known U.S. beauty brand. While we were chatting away about our lives, I asked her, "Do you think there is a difference between American and French women regarding makeup?" Ms. Brown said she saw a big difference. French wear less makeup than Americans. When I asked her if it was a good thing or a bad thing, she told me, "Of course, it's a good thing! French women are more natural. This is the mission of my brand. Natural beauty."

I agree wholeheartedly with Bobbi Brown.

• • •

In Parisian cafés, you can meet people who will become good friends. I met Shauna when I gave a lecture about Simone de Beauvoir, the French feminist. Shauna is American and when I met her, she had just arrived in Paris from New York.

We clicked immediately. When she told me, she used to be a Flamenco dancer, I could not help telling her, "I look more like a Spanish flamenco dancer than you! You look like an Irish dancer!"

She burst out laughing. Shauna is in her late fifties and she is the stereotypical vision of an Irish woman: red hair with pale skin, beautiful green eyes, and a very slender silhouette. One day, she decided to say goodbye to Broadway and make her dream come true: living in Paris. It wasn't easy, of course, since she spoke not a word of French, had no job, no family, and no friends. But she managed it, and I really admire her. We became good friends. She cheers me up when I'm down and being too negative about myself. Shauna never gives up, so she is my "you can do it" role model.

This is why I like American women. They use the sisterhood concept that we French women don't have. We are more individualists, I suppose. I have the feeling that American women help each other more.

Since I had one hour before my Hemingway tour for a group of English literature students from Cincinnati, I proposed that Shauna join me for a quick lunch. (Yes, one hour is a quick lunch in France.) We sat on the terrace of Café Descartes in the Latin Quarter, the district of Ancient Romans, and Les Grandes Ecoles, like the Sorbonne.

As we were eating our croque-monsieur, Shauna who was just back from being in New York for two weeks said, "I'm so happy to be back! Paris is my home now. You should see my American friends when I tell them that I live in Paris. They all have stars in their eyes!"

"Oh really?" I asked.

"Yes! It's incredible, the effect Paris has on Americans. It's crazy! But really, when I think about my life in Paris, I don't have the high life that my American friends from New York think I have. For them, living in Paris means eating fabulous, warm croissants every morning, macarons every day with Champagne, shopping on the Champs-Elysées. But I don't have this kind of life. I live in Belleville, which is a working-class neighborhood, and I do nothing special. Look! We just have simple food in an ordinary café, doing nothing special. But Americans think I have the dreamy life and they all envy me. I like my life here, but my American friends would probably be disappointed if they lived my Paris life."

"Well, Belleville is not a bad area," I say smiling. "It's my home. As you know, I was born in Belleville. I like Belleville because It's a popular and alive district with cobblestoned streets. It's the sepia-toned Paris of Edith Piaf. It's also a cosmopolitan place. Belleville is like a millefeuille. There are layers of different cultures: French, Arabic, Jewish, Chinese and at last the BOurgeois BOhemian, aka, Bobo. But do you like this ordinary life ? I mean, doing nothing special in Belleville?"

"Oh! I love it!" Shauna says. "This is the life I always wanted to live. Doing nothing special in Paris. You know Americans always have to 'do' things. We have to have plans and goals, otherwise you're seen as a loser. And in New York it's even worse. When you meet up with a friend, you have to talk about all the things you're doing. Americans live in the future. You need to have goals to achieve."

"Oh really?" I answer Shauna. "I like New-York because It's a city which gives you energy. But I'm glad to live in Paris, maybe because I'm a bit lazy. It's true that here we enjoy the moment, the present. But I don't agree with you, Shauna. Your life in Paris is not ordinary, at all. It's a simple life, not a luxury life—yes—but it's a good life. "Plus," I say, "we're not in an ordinary café. Look at the name! It's Café Descartes from the first modern philosopher René Descartes, who lived in the 17th century. And look there!" I point to an old stone wall visible from where we are sitting. Shauna turns her head to look.

"This is the old wall of Philip Auguste," I say, "built in the 12th century to protect Paris from the English. Where else could you eat inexpensive, delicious lunch in a place named for a famous 17th century philosopher while admiring a 12th century wall?"

"Only in Paris," Shauna says, smiling.

"And I don't even mention the fact that Hemingway lived fifty meters from where we are. So, no, you are not living an ordinary life in Paris, Shauna! You live an authentic life in Paris!"

"You're right." Shauna says. "You know, the thing I like the most here is that I feel more myself. I feel free. New York is a free city too, of course. I left California for New York to have a free life. But New York is more masculine than Paris. Do you remember the words of the Sinatra song, New York, New York? 'If I can make it there, I'll make it anywhere?' You have to work a lot in New-York. Paris is a more sensual city, softer. Everything is done for pleasure here, to enjoy the little pleasures of life. Paris is a feminine city."

"Yes, Paris is a feminine city," I agree. "I would even add that Paris is a woman. That's why all women feel comfortable in Paris. My girlfriends from all over the world who've lived in Paris have told me the same thing. Eun-Jong the Korean architect, Momoko the illustrator from Japan, Ana-Sofia the Colombian engineer, Manisha, the housewife from India, and Alexandra, the Italian teacher from Russia—they all live in Paris and they all told me they've felt freer here. Paris made them become the woman they wanted to be. I call this phenomenon 'The Paris Effect.'"

"Exactly," Shauna said. "I'm a new woman since I've lived in Paris. In Paris, I never feel invisible. Here men check me out. Even when I'm not at my best, French men look at me. I feel more feminine in Paris. You know, it sounds incredible, but I've met the best men of my life here. And it was when I was looking awful."

"Awful? What do you mean? You don't look awful!"

"I mean when I was hiking in the Fontainebleau forest with hundreds of people. Each time I met a charming French man who was extremely nice and wanted to invite me for a coffee later. In the U.S., I never flirted when I was hiking!"

"Lucky girl!" Then I told her I was jealous. "I want to hike in the forest and meet some men! You think you looked awful, but that's according to your American standards, not French ones. You don't look awful at all, even when you're wearing your hiking clothes." I told Shauna she'd become a true "Parisienne."

After our lunch, as I was waiting for my American students, I started thinking about the discussion I'd had with Shauna. Who is a Parisian woman and who is not? And what does it mean to be a 'true' Parisian woman? Is Shauna a Parisienne or is she an American woman who lives in Paris? And do you need to live in Paris to feel the Paris Effect? Like love at first sight, can your life be changed just as much if you've visited Paris just once?

I had fifteen minutes before my group arrived, so I crossed the street to look at some books in the window of a bookshop. There were many biographies. A book on Sacha Guitry caught my eye. Oh! I know the author of this book! It's Henry Gidel, who I met at Café de Flore in Saint-Germain-des-Prés a few months before.

I was sitting upstairs in the café. By the way, tourists like to sit on the terrace of Café de Flore, but the true Parisians prefer à l'étage—upstairs—or as we call it, the first floor. When I saw a book about Coco Chanel on the table of the man next to me, I could not resist asking him if the book was good or not.

"I'm the author," he told me. "So, I suppose it's an excellent book." He gave me a playful smile.

We started to chat. He was a delightful mature Parisian man. So delicate and refined. He was waiting for a friend to give him his new "excellent" biography on Chanel.

As I was drinking my coffee, Henry and I talked about Coco Chanel.

"I'm the only biographer of Chanel who had free access to the Chanel archives," he told me.

Incredible. So, you can imagine that all the unanswered questions I had about Chanel were answered by Henry that day.

Henry also told me that he was a theater historian, and that he'd won the prestigious Goncourt award in 1995 for his biography of Sacha Guitry. (The Goncourt is one of the most prestigious literary awards in France.) He had been doing lecture tours about Guitry on luxury yachts on the Danube. I told him he was living my dream life: to be well paid to do lecture tours about French history on yachts.

Since his friend never came to the café, he offered the Chanel book to me. What an exquisite man! I was as happy as a little girl on her birthday.

As I stood looking at Henry's award-winning biography of Guitry in the shop window, I realize I have to buy it. And I do like Sacha Guitry. Born in Saint-Petersburg in 1885, Guitry had not only a brilliant mind but a comedic one, too. He was a creative movie director, and a playwright. Even now, his plays are very popular in France. This talented artist is one of the best representatives of the Parisian wit.

In 1921, the first radio broadcast went out over French airwaves. This broadcast was made where the highest radio antenna was located: at the top of the Eiffel Tower. For the first time, the French could hear a human voice on a radio. Which actor was invited for this unique radio show? Who was as famous as the Eiffel Tower in the 1920s? Which French comedian had a voice you could immediately recognize? Sacha Guitry, of course. It's Guitry and his beautiful wife, Yvonne Printemps, who all the French people heard for the first time, sitting in their homes. Guitry was ironic, elegant, witty, seductive, entertaining, charming, smart, and silly all at the same time. Exactly my type of man. Too bad I never met him.

Sacha Guitry. It's he who answered my question about what makes you Parisian. In a few brilliant words, Guitry describes the Paris Effect perfectly:

"Being a Parisian is not about being born in Paris, it is about being reborn there." —Sacha Guitry (1885-1957)

Chapter 10:

The Art of Seduction

HOW DID I SEDUCE MISTER CEO? HOW DID I CHARM THE Alpha Male who had everything in life? Everyone has their own way to seduce. I'm not going to teach you how to seduce men because I'm sure you're already charming, with your own little secrets to mesmerize a man. But I can tell you about something else: something sparkling and joyful. The Art of Seduction. It might sound old-fashioned and retro to you, but French women still love the game of seduction.

Tip #1: Love is not about work.

I had never before met a man like Mister CEO. He could buy absolutely everything he wanted. When he liked a house or a flat anywhere in the world, he bought it. Plus boats, cars—two cars, a BMW convertible for when it's sunny, and a Jaguar for when it's raining. I've already told you about the very expensive watches. When I was with Mister CEO, I was aware the level of the beauty I was competing with was very high because he could have the most beautiful, seductive women he wanted.

Erik was not only rich, but he was also very charming. He was like Louis XIV, the glorious French King from the 17th century. Louis the

XIV, AKA The Sun King, was handsome, charming, rich and powerful. The most beautiful women in the French kingdom wanted to have an affair with the Sun King. Same with Mister CEO. Plenty of perfect women wanted the King of Silicon Valley. I know, because he told me…much later. Plus, there was Barbara, his attractive assistant. Compared to Barbara I looked chubby, not trendy, and not modern at all. And unfortunately, I did not have her budget to buy her expensive, fashionable clothes—or the slim model's frame to show them off. Since I knew I was not perfect, I needed to consider what skills I did have to seduce my charming prince.

How? I was myself. I didn't play the perfect woman because compared to the alluring American woman, I was not perfect. I didn't even try to be perfect. I did not want to look artificial, to be someone who was not me. So, I didn't play too hard. When it comes to love, French women are lazy. So, I didn't do too much. I tried to be me, but better. Just not the "perfect" me. For a date, a party, or fancy dinner, I never put on too much makeup. I don't wear overly sophisticated clothes, either. It's my "Oh, it will be enough!" rule. I mean, I try to look presentable, but I never try to be Miss World. A date is not a beauty competition. Of course, I made efforts to seduce Mister CEO but I didn't try to look sexy. I wanted to exude elegance and charm. Why? Because I didn't want to be a woman I was not: a very sophisticated woman with lots of makeup and tight clothes. Don't get me wrong; I have nothing against very feminine women, but it's not me. I never wear short skirts, so I didn't wear a short skirt to show off my legs, or a top with a plunging neckline either, because I don't like to show my breasts too openly. I prefer to be subtle. Illusion is more effective on the imagination. In other words, I was wearing clothes I liked, not clothes he would have liked. I wore clothes I usually wear: a pencil skirt with a top, a nice jacket, and high-heeled boots. Same with the makeup: I didn't over-indulge; just some lipstick and mascara. I was me with a little bit more effort, but still me, still moi.

You will be irresistible if you are yourself.

Don't forget that perfection is not only artificial, but boring. How can you show your personality if you're perfect? Perfection also scares men. Don't think your date is not scared by you, because he is. And which man would like to have a date with Wonder Woman? You'll be stressed out trying to be perfect, and he will be stressed out because he'll be intimidated by you. If you're a little bit messy, you're fine, because you'll appear more accessible. You'll be more human and more authentic. Where is your charm if you look like a supermodel at Fashion Week?

Think about your message. Clothes give off a nonverbal message. If you're too sexy, your message to your date will be: I want to seduce you. He will take it for granted; he won't make any effort. Why should he? He'll think the perfect woman in front of him is saying "I want you, so I spent two hours making myself perfect for you." Me, I never let a man think anything is for granted. Never. I didn't want Mister CEO to think I'd made an effort just for him. I made an effort, yes, but it was subtle. Again my, "It will be enough" rule. Much later, Mister CEO told me the first thing he appreciated about me was the fact I was not artificial. He told me he liked me because I was genuine. He also insisted on the fact I was not trying to seduce him. Of course, I was trying to seduce him. but he didn't guess that was my objective because I never outwardly showed him.

Don't show a man you are trying to seduce him. Because the key to seduction is not to show you your hand.

Tip #2: Embrace the high heels effect.

When you want to live La Vie Parisienne (the Parisian life) you try to be invited to as many parties as you can. Once, I was at a dinner organized by American expats in Paris. It was summer so I was wearing a dress with black high-heeled sandals. While sipping my glass of Champagne on the balcony, I met two Americans: a man and a woman. The man was much older than the woman.

He was an attractive lawyer in his sixties from California, all in white: a white linen shirt and trousers. He struck me as a Robert Redford look-alike, so you can guess he was not at all ugly. Plus, he was very friendly, and always smiling. The woman was half his age, in her thirties. She was nice, too. He mentioned many times that she was his girlfriend. He seemed very proud to have caught such a fresh, young woman. I remember that she was wearing a short blue dress with flat black boots. During our conversation, the Californian Robert Redford look-alike made a comment about my shoes. He told me I shouldn't wear high heels because it was bad for my back and my feet.

I replied with a smile that my back and feet were fine, thank you, but the Californian lawyer started to make his arguments; he told me he was a true feminist, and if women were wearing high-heeled shoes it was only to please men. Then he added, I should not damage my health just to seduce men. He said he felt very sorry for me. To prove his point, he motioned toward his tall girlfriend, and declared that I should imitate her, and wear flat shoes.

I was annoyed, of course.

"If I'm wearing high heels, it's because I like high heels, not to seduce a man," I said. I didn't want to be unfriendly, but on the inside I was screaming: If you're such a feminist, why are you dictating to me what kind of shoes I should be wearing?

I smiled and kept calm, refrained from voicing my internal dialogue because I didn't want to cause a scene with the Robert Redford look alike.

His young girlfriend had no opinion about the point in question. To be honest, I didn't like her plain, flat shoes, but I certainly couldn't say that, either. It's not polite.

As darkness fell, it began to get cold. I left the terrace, and the Californian couple, to go inside the warm apartment. I sat on a sofa and started to chat with other nice American. They were telling me how lucky I was to live in such a beautiful city. Then "Robert Redford" came inside – alone. He sat right next to me; I could feel his eyes on me, watching me as I conversed with his compatriots. I turned slightly and saw he was staring at my high-heeled sandals. I thought, "Please, not again." If he starts one more time with his heavy feminist speech about my shoes, I'll be a lot less friendly.

I was about to tell him to give me a break about the high heels when I heard him sigh. He sidled up close to me and whispered in my ear, "I really like your shoes. You look wonderful."

I couldn't say a word because I could not stop laughing. Et voilà!

You don't need me to preach that you can be feminine and a feminist. Of course, you don't need to wear high heels to be a woman. Your femininity is not in your shoes. If you feel good wearing sneakers, it's perfectly fine. Me? I feel miserable in sneakers. High heels have an effect. First, high heels have an effect on me. I'm nicer in high heels. I feel nicer, so I feel more confident when I wear them. Therefore, I feel more powerful.

You don't move your body the same way when you wear high-heeled shoes, because you're more graceful. The key to seduction is to feel confident. So, try high heels and you'll see the effect on you—and you'll see the effect on the Robert Redfords out there, too.

Tip #3: Have a signature scent.

Perfume is a way to express your personality. It's your signature. Olfactive sense is another way to seduce, another nonverbal tool in the parlance of love.

A good perfume is a magical filter. I always have a small sample of my perfume in my bag. With my perfume in my bag, I can bring my own world everywhere—the 1920s world. My perfume was quite effective with Mister CEO. He appreciated my powdered vanilla fragrance. I'm sure he did sniff at his blue woolen scarf all evening after I left him. If my perfume worked with the austere Mister CEO, it's because perfume stirs emotion. It worked so well that he gifted me the huge bottle of Habanita, my favorite perfume. A man will be reminded of you even when you're not with him, thanks to your fragrance.

Perfume is very important to the French. Women, men, and even children, wear perfume in France. I offered my two sons their first fragrance—a light lemon scent—at age 6. When they turned 16, they did not want me to choose for them any longer, so they bought their own perfumes.

France historically is the world leader of perfumes. In the 18th century at Versailles, the Louis XV court was called La Cour Parfumée, the perfumed court, because all the courtesans had to wear a new scent every day. Despite modern-day beliefs, it was not to hide the bad body odors, because by this era, hygiene was becoming important in France. It's because it was chic to be perfumed. After Louis XV, it's Marie Antoinette who promoted the fresh French fragrances. Then Napoléon used to bring liters of eau de cologne on the battlefields to splash his highly groomed body. Some people state that he needed 43 liters a day. It's not a coincidence that Napoleon's scent is one of oldest French brand perfume: Jean-Marie Farina by Roger et Gallet since 1862. But the oldest French perfume brand is Guerlain, since 1828. Ah, Guerlain! Have you ever smelled L'Heure Bleue? (I have one bottle at home) Or the iconic Shalimar? Just the names take you back to a time of elegant refinement.

The perfume capital is the city of Grasse located in the south of France, near Nice. Since 1714, all the famous French perfumes have been made here. Dior, Yves Saint Laurent, and Chanel all make their prestigious fragrances there. Even the famous Chanel No. 5 was created in Grasse. Habanita, my beloved scent, was created in this perfumed city, too. Both Chanel No. 5 and Habanita were created in the same year, 1921, but one is more famous than the other.

A perfume expresses your personality. Find a perfume that is you and own it, because your perfume is you! Perfume can create strong feelings. Maybe some people won't like your perfume in the same way there will always be people who won't like your personality. They'll complain it's too strong, too sweet, too much; that it bothers them, or that they have an allergy. A Canadian woman explained to me that in her country it's forbidden to wear perfume on public buses. And in a television documentary about Grasse and the perfume industry, I learned that in some American universities, students are not even allowed to spray perfume on themselves in public. In America, many company buildings have set up scent-free zones.

I understand that a strong perfume can bother someone. One evening, I was eating in a restaurant in the Trocadero neighborhood near the Eiffel Tower with Ron, my good friend from New York.

Well, I was trying to eat, but in fact I was suffocating. The woman at the next table had not mastered the way to wear her Hypnotic Poison by Dior. Her perfume was really too strong.

I asked to be moved to another table, but the restaurant was full. I had many murderous thoughts towards this woman because her perfume was invading my private space. Scent is important, but it's also important to not impose your perfume on those around you! I also understand and have experienced first-hand how perfume can bother another's olfactory sense. I've never been told my perfume was too strong because when I apply it, I'm careful to perfume myself and not others.

Still, why do I have to stop putting on my perfume because of a minority? To forbid any smell in public spaces—isn't it somewhat excessive? I call this phenomenon the dictatorship of the minority. I'm very sorry for people who have any perfume allergy, and I'm delighted that in France we worship perfumes.

For many French artists through the ages, perfume was more than an accessory; it was the key for the seduction. Many poems and books have been written about the power of a woman's perfume. Charles Baudelaire, the great French poet from the 19th century, wrote many poems dedicated to perfume in "The Flowers of Devil." Baudelaire tells, better than me, how perfume has a magical effect, a power to charm. An intoxicating perfume is the language of your soul, but it can be an erotic weapon, too.

It's well known that a specific smell or taste has the power to recall an event from your past. It's called "the reminiscence effect." You recognize a smell, and suddenly you're flooded with a memory: the perfume of your adored mother or a fond childhood memory, for example. Marcel Proust, arguably the greatest French writer from the 20th century, wrote about this phenomenon. It's the most famous episode from his novel in seven parts, "In Search of the Lost Time." To sum up, Marcel Proust, who lived in Paris, caught a cold. He felt miserable, so to cheer himself up, he had tea with a madeleine (a delicate miniature sponge cake). The moment he dipped his cake into the tea and—bam!—he was happy again. But why? he wondered. What changed his mood so quickly? Suddenly, he realized: it was the taste of the madeleine dipped in tea. This specific taste reminded him of his happy childhood in the countryside. His Aunt Léonie always gave him a madeleine dipped in her herbal tea. All the memories of his carefree youth appeared in his cup of tea. From a madeleine dipped in his tea, Marcel Proust invented neuroscience.

Your perfume will touch the sensitive side of a man's brain. A good perfume is a love poem. Coco Chanel said, "A woman without perfume has no future." Indeed, she was right—even if she did appropriate this famous quote from the French poet, Paul Valéry. Poets are always right; they see and feel things that we ordinary human beings don't.

So, if you want to be a woman with a bright future, do as the poet tells you and put on some perfume!

Tip #4: Know the courtesan's secret.

Once upon a time, there was a famous French courtesan born in Paris. Her name was Anne de Lenclos, but everyone called her "Ninon." She was born in 1672 and lived in the Marais. Anne was beautiful, educated, and refined. The most magnificent courtesan of them all, Ninon de Lenclos, could seduce young men even when she was 70 years old.

This was in the 17th century and women didn't go to school. They couldn't marry the man of their own choosing. And if their parents didn't have a dowry for their daughter, she was sent to a convent at the age of five to live there until her death.

Ninon's mother attempted to send her to a convent, but Ninon said "non!" She said non to the convent. She said non to God. She said non to the wedding. She said non to the family. Ninon de Lenclos decided to be free in a century that did not allow freedom for women. She chose the life of a courtesan—but not a "cheap" one. Thanks to her beauty and intelligence, she became the most fashionable courtesan of the French kingdom—and, shall we say, the most expensive. I know what you are thinking. How could you admire a woman selling herself to make a life? But remember, it was a long time ago. It was her only choice.

One of her lovers bought her a mansion in the Marais, one of the most prestigious neighborhoods in Paris at that time. The free spirit Ninon decided that she would choose her clients—and that she would leave instead of being left. She had three kinds of men: 1) The Payers who paid a minimum of 500 Louis (3,500 US dollars) to have an intimate conversation with her in the cozy yellow bedroom; 2) The Martyrs, those waiting to perhaps become a Payer one day, and 3) The Favorites, who were the men she chose and loved—and who did not pay. The romantic Ninon became the love coach to all the noble knights—fathers and sons. She taught them how to behave with a woman in a salon…and in bed.

Ninon de Lenclos is the first woman who used language as an erotic tool. She had her own literary salon where it was compulsory to be witty, and arrogance was strictly forbidden. These literary salons were the only place where women could have power. Famous women of the age such as Catherine de Rambouillet, and the writer Madame de La Fayette who created the most refined literary salons in Paris. While men were still using Latin, the women, who did not know Latin, spoke only in French. The Parisian women of the 17th century, through their elegant literary salons, enriched and modernized the French language. If you had the privilege to be invited by Ninon to attend her fashionable salon (between the hours of 5 pm and 7 pm), you would have been offered a lovely cup of violet tea (her favorite beverage), or a hot chocolate from the first chocolate shop of Paris (and the price of that chocolate was nearly a week's salary for a Parisian worker). You would have made jokes with Molière, and Jean-Baptiste Lully, the first musician to the court of Louis XIV, would have played a magical baroque aria for you.

French women invented the subtle art of conversation and the code of gallantry between men and women, both concepts still very important in French society.

The aristocracy from Paris wondered how Ninon could stay looking so young and attractive. At 60 years old, she could still easily pass for a woman of 40. In the 17th century, a woman of 40 was already considered very old. But not Ninon, who stayed slim and fresh all her life, thanks to a strict diet. When people were drinking heavy wine and spicy food, Ninon was eating light fare and drinking only water.

People of that area thought water caused disease, so they did not wash, and the smell was quite obvious! But not Ninon. She took baths, and slathered rosewater and almond oil on her sensual body. While the crème de la crème of Parisian women hid their spots and blemishes behind well-placed scarves and faux beauty marks, Ninon had a spotless, porcelain complexion.

She had her little beauty secrets, of course, that you can still find on the Internet. It's quite easy, actually: apply a mixture of onion juice, almond oil, and "spermicia." What's spermicia, you ask? Whale sperm. But don't worry, if you can't find whale sperm at Walmart, you can use beeswax, instead. Fortunately, now we don't have to smell like onion or whale sperm to have nice skin.

Of course, in the 17th century, you could not live the life of a scandalous woman without having your share of troubles. She was sent to a convent twice on the orders of Anne of Austria (the regent mother of Louis XIV) because she was living too openly as a libertine. Fortunately, a distinguished member of her fan club included the incredible Queen Christina of Sweden, who had her set free.

Before dying at the ripe old age of 85 on October 17, 1705, Ninon met the young son of her notary, who impressed her so much that she left him money in her will so he could buy books. This intelligent 10-year-old boy was Voltaire.

Why am I talking to you about this famous courtesan from another era? Because the master of the art of seduction is Ninon. She was even the model for the famous courtesans from the 19th century. Two centuries after her death, the successful love goddesses from La Belle Epoque were still imitating her. Why? Because although she was attractive, Ninon was not the most gorgeous woman of her time. But she was the most charming because she understood the gift of conversation. She mastered the art of it. She was also a great listener. She was witty but never arrogant. And she had de l'esprit—spirit. Ninon could talk with men about topics they liked: philosophy, war strategy and hunting, while always staying extremely feminine. It's a mixture that no man can resist—even today.

Everybody likes to talk about themselves, including me. So, with my charming prince, Mister CEO, I was careful not to talk too much about myself, or about my favorite subjects. I made him talk about himself. I listened to him carefully. There will always be women who are younger, slimmer, and more attractive than you. There were plenty of women more beautiful than Ninon de Lenclos, too. But Ninon knew that the body is not enough. When you want to seduce, you need to have spirit. Even the allure of the sexiest woman won't last forever if she's dull.

It gives one hope. I seduced Mister CEO thanks to my art of conversation. I purposefully challenged his brain because men like to be intellectually stimulated. Ninon was doing this, too. I didn't talk about food, taxes, his job, his luxury lifestyle, or his ordinary daily life. I talked to him about philosophy, art, history, and literature—things he was not used to talking about. This isn't because he was stupid—far from it. He just wasn't used to intellectual conversations. So, he felt validated. And it was a way to show him I was a well-read woman.

Never hide the intelligent woman inside. French men like smart women because the brain is an erotic tool. Ninon understood this. It's important not to be arrogant or pedantic. So, I tried to be witty, light, and sparkling, exactly like Mademoiselle de Lenclos. Mister CEO confessed to me later that he is often bored, but with me, he was never bored.

How to master the art of conversation like a courtesan? How to be at ease when you speak with a perfect stranger? Be open, read books. Any books (comic books don't count!). Go to your library—it's cheap and there are many subjects to learn about. Listen to cultural radio programs or watch them on YouTube. I never do the dishes without listening to a cultural podcast.

I'm not saying you need to be an expert in Gilles Deleuze, the famous French philosopher who belongs to the schools of Post-Structuralism, Materialism, and Neo-Spinozism. (I hope I impressed you! To be honest, when I read Deleuze, I wonder if I really speak French because I don't understand a word.) No, you don't need to be an intellectual to master the art of conversation. Always ask yourself questions. Stay curious. For example, have you noticed that dinner knives are rounded at the tip? This comes from Richelieu, the first minister of Louis XIII. Era of Ninon. Richelieu was tired of men using the sharp-tipped knives to clean their teeth at table. He found it disgusting, so he created a law to make rounded knives. Next time you're at a dinner party, you'll have something to talk about with the stranger next to you.

Be curious about what you like; feed your brain as much as you moisturize your skin. Read as much as you use lipsticks. If you train your brain as much as you train your body, you'll be a successful seducer. You will seduce only smart and decent men, not the mediocre.

To sum up, if you want to seduce a man, don't show him you're interested; show him you are interesting.

Tip #5: Be mysterious.

In France, blind dates are not really popular. I don't like blind dates. In ten minutes, the perfect stranger in front of you will know everything about your life: your job (or the fact you don't have a job), your degrees, your university, if you're divorced, if you're poor or rich, your favorite vacation spot, if you're the world skiing champion, etc., etc., etc.. Because you want to impress your date, I'm sure you might exaggerate your skills, be tempted to brag about yourself. But to brag has the exact opposite effect you are going for. Bragging provokes repulsion, not seduction. For me, a blind date is a mixture of a job interview and a self-promotion. Yikes!

To seduce, you need to be a little mysterious. It's like a movie. If you already know the ending in the first ten minutes—spoiler alert—where is the pleasure in that? Where is the suspense? This joy is in the discovery of the personality of the characters.

Being mysterious about your skills is very important. If you're fluent in Spanish for example, undersell it: "Oh, me? I can only speak a few words." Because when he finds out later that you actually speak Spanish like a fla-menco dancer from Seville, he will be impressed. In seduction, you have to surprise a man. It's important not to be in a hurry. Take your time, because if you're too quick, you'll ruin your chances of seduction. For example, if you are a great singer, don't say you're the new Céline Dion. Just say, "I really love to sing." That's it. Don't tell him you performed at Carnegie Hall, even if (I hope) for you it's true. Wait for the moment that you'll be able to sing, then you'll see the effect on him.

The difficulty is how and when to bring about the moment for your charming prince to discover your skill. Be patient; it will come. For exam-ple, if you are a good cook, never say you're a chef. It's boasting unneces-sarily, and it's already been explained that this is the enemy of seduction. Just say you like cooking. He'll quickly realize you probably have a French soul to be able to cook so well. Your moment will arrive; don't worry. Don't show him that you're proud of yourself, even if I'm sure you have excellent reasons to be proud of yourself. Bragging is very childish. You're a wise woman; if you feel good about yourself you don't need to brag.

With Mister CEO, it was difficult to impress him because he trav-elled everywhere and knew so many things. So, I thought I could impress him with the foreign languages I spoke. But I found my moment. Do you remember the story of the restaurant with the couple from China at the table next to us? I never told him I could speak (a bit of) Chinese. When he asked me where I learned Chinese, I never told him I sweat blood and tears to learn how to speak, write, and read Mandarin. I let him think it was easy for me, and always stayed humble. The less you say about your skills (everybody has skills) the more impressed he will be when he discovers them.

You have to be mysterious about your love life, too. I never mentioned to Mister CEO if I was available or not. Maybe I was…maybe I wasn't. I never disclosed intimate facts about myself (except that I had kids); I never talked about my emotional or romantic life—not about a husband, boyfriend, or lovers. I was mute about my love life, on purpose. Like a spy, I kept my life a secret.

I flirted (again, on purpose) with the waiter in front of Mister CEO. I was extra sweet and witty with our waiter, and he became extra nice with me, too—complimenting me. Of course, that was the goal. I did give Mister CEO attention, but I let him know my eyes were not focused on him all the time. Of course, this wasn't true, because my eyes were focused on him, but I wanted him to realize other men could be attracted to me, and I to them. (By the way, don't forget to give a generous tip to the friendly waiter afterward.)

Tip #6: Remember that you are a diva!

Let your inner diva shine. Let him admire you in all your glory. You are not his best friend, so he does not need to learn you are on a diet. By the way, you are not on a diet, instead you are a poetical woman who is not interested in material things such as food. Love and water feed you. The same applies to everything that's not romantic. You'll have plenty of time to tell him after the seduction that you have particular allergies and that you never finish a book with more than two hundred pages. Or that your parents divorced when you were four, which prompted a nervous breakdown. You are not a depressed woman or a weird woman who talks to herself sometimes. You are a sensitive, mystical woman who likes to talk with the angels.

Tip #7: The Power of The Voice

I never understood why Americans speak so loudly. Well, in fact, I think I know why. Because America is a big country. Since America is a big country, you have to shout or no one will hear you. France is a small country, about the size of Texas. Therefore, French people have to whisper when they speak otherwise everybody would hear what they say. Even if you're very happy, you're not obliged to scream "Oh my God!" every five minutes.

Nothing is less seductive than looking like an excited teenager. You're a mature woman who is the master of her emotions. Try to use words to express your incredible joy but don't speak loudly. The reason not to shout is so that he leans. People listen more when you don't yell. When I was with Mister CEO, I was careful to have a deep voice and I never shouted. My models are the radio announcers on the Parisian station France Inter Paris.

In 2017, the co-founder of Twitter, Jack Dorsey, said FIP is the best radio station in the world, and that's why he listened to it so much. I can't agree more. I've listened to FIP since I was 12. On FIP there is only music, all kinds of music: French pop songs, classical music, jazz, blues, world music. And from time to time, you can hear those sensual voices giving you the traffic report, talking about cultural events. When Erik and I were in the taxi on the way to the bridge that night, the sensual voice of the women of FIP rode along with us. These radio announcers are famous for being the most seductive of all the French radio stations. It's difficult to describe to you the melody of those voices. Listen to FIP on the Internet and you'll understand what I mean.

If you are too shy to sing, you can learn poetry. If you recite a beautiful poem, slowly in a soft voice, it's fine too. The magical charm will work!

Epilogue

WITH THE COVID THINGS HAVE CHANGED IN THE WORLD. Paris has changed too. Paris was deserted. Paris was quiet, too quiet. But fortunately things became a bit normal again. I was so moved to have my first coffee at Café de Flore when the curfew was over. What could I tell you more about my beloved city? I know. I wish you to see and breathe Paris's air one day, to have a coffee on a Paris Café's terrace one day and doing nothing except watch the world go by and feed your soul. Because as a famous French writer said:

"A breath of Paris preserves the soul." —Victor Hugo (1802-1885)

Merci!

I WARMLY THANK ALL THE PEOPLE WHO INSPIRED ME AND helped me: Chrissy from Seattle who convinced me I was able to write in English, Lisa A who helped me with my English, Reg C, Shauna, Jean P from Corsica, Marie-Jeanne Colombani, Michel V, Henry Gidel, Bobbi Brown, Jamie Cat Callan, John from England, Peter from Sweden, Ariel from Israël, Ron, Carla, Soumeya, Yaëlle, Micheline my mother in law, Didier N, Stéphane M, Jérôme C, Terrance, Jeremy & Isabelle my American cousins from Baltimore, Julia, Lilianne, Karine, Karen, Sophie, Janet, Andrew Lear, Ted Belton the great photographer from Canada, Mark Werb for my book-cover, Dominique, Rosemary, Alexandra, Manisha, Eun-Jong, Ana-Sofia, Momoko, Barbara, Jacky. Merci to my beloved sons Ethan and Elias, my parents Boris and Sarah and Daphné my sister.